AF598896

CLASSIC GUNS OF THE WORLD SERIES

THE STEN

The Legendary World War II British Submachine Gun

LUC GUILLOU

THE STEN

The Legendary World War II British Submachine Gun

CLASSIC GUNS OF THE WORLD SERIES

LANCHESTER

MK.I & MK.I*

MK.II & MK.III

MK.5

FOREIGN VARIANTS

ACCESSORIES

Schiffer Publishing Ltd®
4880 Lower Valley Road • Atglen, PA 19310

Originally published as *La Sten: L'Arme de la Résistance* by RÉGI Arm,
Paris © 2015 RÉGI Arm
Translated from the French by Julia and Frédéric Finel

Library of Congress Control Number: 2017953841

Cover design by Justin Watkinson
Type set in Helvetica Neue LT Pro/Times New Roman

ISBN: 978-0-7643-5485-4
Printed in China

Published by Schiffer Publishing, Ltd.
4880 Lower Valley Road
Atglen, PA 19310
Phone: (610) 593-1777; Fax: (610) 593-2002
E-mail: Info@schifferbooks.com
Web: www.schifferbooks.com

CONTENTS

INTRODUCTION

A DISARMED KINGDOM

A group of sailors of the *Kriegsmarine* look at the huge quantity of equipment abandoned by the British Expeditionary Force in France before its hurried re-embarkation for Great Britain. *ECPAD*

Maj. Gen. Sir Colin McVean Gubbins. Winston Churchill put this officer, whose life story resembles that of an adventure novel, in charge of organizing the auxiliary units of the Home Guard. His experience of the secret war was to make him one of the orchestrators of the SOE; the service responsible for supporting resistance movements in occupied countries.

The German Army offensive of May 1940, crushed the French Army in six weeks and pressured the small expeditionary force sent to France by the British into a hurried re-embarkation, its equipment and weapons having to be abandoned in order to save the maximum number of men. The capitulation of France, following on from the crushing of Poland, Denmark and Norway, Belgium, and the Netherlands, left Great Britain to face Germany alone.

Sweat, Blood, and Tears

Having failed to force Great Britain to sign a peace treaty, Adolf Hitler decided to prepare for the invasion of the British Isles. Previously, in order for German troops to cross the Channel, the Royal Air Force (RAF) had to be destroyed, giving Hitler total mastery of the skies and so enabling him to protect his landing fleet from the powerful Royal Navy.

Reichsmarschall Hermann Göring was committed to destroying the RAF and undermining the morale of the British nation by carrying out a pitiless bombing campaign, at the same time as the *Wehrmacht* prepared for invasion and the *Kriegsmarine* ensured a fierce blockade of the British Isles to prevent any further importation of both raw materials and weapons from the US or nations of the British Empire.

The Battle of Britain forms the aerial part of this preparatory phase of the invasion and the Battle of the Atlantic naval part. As we know now, the *Luftwaffe* could neither destroy the RAF nor break the spirit of resistance of the British people.

From the summer of 1940, Winston Churchill, Prime Minister of Great Britain, entrusted to Col. Colin Gubbins the task of organizing the foundations of resistance to the German invasion. Gubbins, who had served in Russia during the civil war before being posted to Ireland and the Middle East, possessed a solid experience in secret and subversive warfare.

He organized British resistance into two parts; groups of locals, whose sole mission was to observe German troops and to identify possible targets before transmitting the information to the second component, "action" groups known under the intentionally insignificant term "auxiliary units," made up of a dozen men selected from the particularly dynamic individuals of the Home Guard.

Some rifles, saved during the re-embarkation of British Expeditionary Force, are carefully retrieved by evacuated troops landing in Ramsgate in June 1940, exhausted but alive! *DR*

A German officer talking to a "Bobby." This photo, widely distributed by German propaganda, was taken in the Channel Islands, the only part of British territory to be occupied by the *Wehrmacht*. This represented the nightmare for many British subjects, who had escaped foreign occupation since William the Conqueror. *DR*

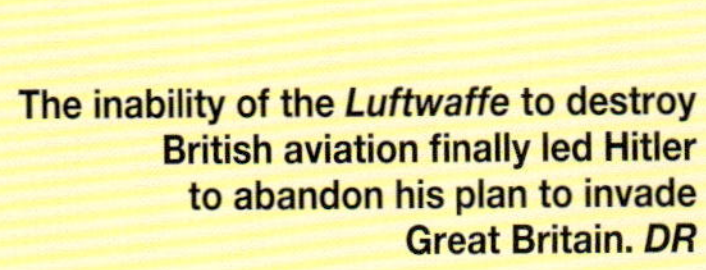

The inability of the *Luftwaffe* to destroy British aviation finally led Hitler to abandon his plan to invade Great Britain. *DR*

The men chosen were most often those who were robust, determined, and used to living in the countryside, such as foresters or gamekeepers. The "action" groups, who had hiding places as well as means of transmitting by radio, were equipped with modern weapons adapted to guerilla warfare: explosives, anti-tank and incendiary devices, weapons with silencers and submachine guns. No weapon of this type was being manufactured in Great Britain at that time, it was necessary to urgently order huge quantities of Thompsons as well as Smith & Wesson semi-automatic rifles from the United States.

Not succeeding in gaining mastery of the skies, vital for undertaking the invasion of Great Britain, Hitler eventually abandoned this plan and settled for simply instructing his U-boat fleet to ensure the sea blockade and, in so doing, weakened the country by preventing any supplies arriving from overseas. The Battle of Britain was to be followed by the Battle of the Atlantic.

After the threat of a German invasion was ruled out, the Home Guard donated their Thompsons to the British Army. They were then used by combat units in North Africa and commandos in combined operations. *DR*

Thompson Submachine Guns

As early as 1940, a British purchasing commission was sent to the United States with the imperative mission of acquiring as many Lockheed Hudson anti-submarine combat planes and submachine guns as possible. The commission turned to the Thompson, the only submachine gun available on the American market. An order totaling 300,000 Thompson submachine guns and 249 million .45 cartridges was placed.

The laws of neutrality then applied by the United States authorized the sale of weapons to a country at war on condition that they were paid for immediately and that their new owners took care of their transport (the "Cash and Carry" law). The payment included a third of gold reserves and the various assets available in the United States. It cost the British treasury a small fortune.

The first Thompson submachine guns delivered to Great Britain were Savage made 1928 models with a vertical front grip. This example is mounted with a twenty-round magazine with viewing holes covered by tin to prevent sand penetrating the magazine during operations in sandy terrain such as deserts or beaches. In accordance with established British practice, the sling ring has been transferred to the top of the butt, itself reinforced by two cross screws, and the joint between the butt and the weapon has been tightened to avoid swinging. Consequently, the butts are no longer interchangeable from one weapon to the other, so the metal base of the butt has been stamped with a number to make sure the correct butt was kept with its corresponding weapon during group disassembly. We can see a packet of twelve British made .45 ACP tracer bullet cartridges.

A determined young Army cadet practices firing a Thompson under the watchful eye of an instructor. *DR*

The British Merchant Marine, with the task of ensuring the transport of these weapons to Britain, also paid a heavy price for this mission at a period when German submarines were scouring the Atlantic attempting to reduce British resistance with a merciless sea blockade. Two thirds of Thompsons ordered from the United States ended up at the bottom of the Atlantic, stuck in the cargo ships sunk by the *Kriegsmarine*.

The Thompsons imported into Britain in 1940, were part of the first batch of 1928 models made by the Savage Arms Company. They are marked "MODEL OF 1928" and often bear the British proof stamp. They have a forward pistol grip and were beautifully finished.

Photographs of the period show the British Army frequently used these weapons supplied with fifty-round drum magazines. The regimental armorers frequently added a sling ring (Lee-Enfield or P.14) on the forward pistol grip and transferred the rear sling ring on the top of the butt. It is also common to see two screws added across the butt to stop it from splitting lengthwise.

President Franklin D. Roosevelt, having understood that if Britain were to be defeated the United States would confront the axis powers alone, adopted a law allowing the provision of military equipment to its allies without emptying the coffers. This law, called the Lend-Lease act, translated into the continuation of deliveries to Britain, who no longer needed to pay, as it was from then on a loan for the duration of the war. Unlike the first 1928 model Thompsons delivered to Britain, these weapons bore the same "US ARMY MODEL OF 1928 A1" mark as US Army weapons and, in addition, were stamped with the words "United States Property."

After the surrender of France in June 1940, the United Kingdom, threatened with German invasion and having lost the major part of its infantry weaponry during the French campaign, bought huge amounts of weapons from the United States. The US 17 rifle was part of these emergency purchases carried out in the context of the "Cash and Carry" law in 1940, at the same time as the 1928 model Thompson submachine guns. The Thompson M1A1 would not appear in Britain before 1942, as part of deliveries authorized by the "Lend Lease" law. The gas mask, the air raid warden helmet, and the armband evoke the threat of air raids under which the population had to live during the "Blitz." The shoulder title and the patches of the Home Guard symbolize the resistance that the population was preparing to organize on British soil against German invasion forces. *Collection of the Royal Army Museum of Brussels and Le Poilu of Paris, Photo by Marc de Fromont*

Champion of the resistance, Prime Minister Winston Churchill undertook massive arms purchases from the USA to re-equip the British Army until such time as the national industry was in a position to supply new weapons. A part of the American-bought Thompsons were reserved for the auxiliary units of the Home Guard, who were, in reality, independent resistance sabotage commandos whose task was to organize resistance against the invader. In this photo, Sir Winston has forgotten to lock the bolt to remove the drum magazine. *DR*

A drawing on Capt. Fairbairn's work, *Get Tough!* This book illustrated how to take rapid aim with a 1928 model Thompson. The target is the eternal parachutist!

Transit and storage chest made in Great Britain for the 1928 model Thompson of the Home Guard. These chests contained the weapon and strap, a cleaning kit and some spare parts, five twenty-round magazines, and two fifty-round drum magazines, and could be stored in hide-outs organized by the auxiliary units of the Home Guard to be used in acts of resistance. *Imperial War Museum (IWM) No.FIR6362E*

NOT TO BE PUBLISHED
The information given in this document is not to be communicated, either directly or indirectly, to the Press or to any person not holding an official position in His Majesty's Service.

20
G.S. Publications.
353

Notified in A.C.I. for 3rd July, 1940

Small Arms Training
Volume I, Pamphlet No. 21
Thompson
Sub-Machine-Gun
1940

Crown Copyright Reserved

By Command of the Army Council.

THE WAR OFFICE,
3rd July, 1940.

Printed under the Authority of HIS MAJESTY'S STATIONERY OFFICE by William Clowes & Sons, Ltd., London and Beccles.

British instruction manual for the Thompson submachine gun.

Tea time. A member of the Home Guard cleans his Thompson waiting for the tea to brew. *IWM H 5850*

A Curiosity: Smith & Wesson 1940 Model Semi-Automatic Carbines

Like many private arms manufacturers, the Smith & Wesson Company foresaw that the war raging in Europe would create new needs with regards to weaponry.

The first year of the war, particularly earnest on the French front with a succession of skirmishes between French and German patrols in "No Man's Land," confirmed that a need existed for short-range, rapid-fire weapons. The head engineer of the Smith & Wesson Company, Edward S. Pommeroy, developed a 9 mm caliber parabellum baptized "Smith & Wesson 1940 model semi-automatic sub-carbine," whose patent was issued on September 3, 1940.

The choice to chamber the weapon with a 9 mm parabellum indicates, however, that the weapon was developed for the European market. In those circumstances it could be supposed that Smith & Wesson wanted to sell the automatic submachine gun automatic of its weapon for export and to market another version solely for the American domestic market.

The carbine version was presented to the US Army in November 1939, at the test range in Aberdeen, and sparked no interest whatsoever due to the fact it did not have a .45 ACP chamber and was not capable of firing in bursts!

This short, semi-automatic 9 mm parabellum caliber, functioning with a non-fixed bolt, was so similar to a submachine gun that many collectors were convinced it was one! On the standard version the wooden butt, originally mounted on the prototypes, was replaced by a butt made of Bakelite, which made the carbine considerably lighter.

The weapon bears a safety catch positioned at the rear of the trigger guard and a disassembly lever in front. The bolt handle is in the shape of a hook, like those of the Schmeisser and the Bergman submachine guns. In order to facilitate the cooling of the weapon it is fitted with a thick barrel made lighter by longitudinal grooves.

The Smith & Wesson 1940 model slung across the body. Short, compact, and equipped with a twenty round magazine, the weapon could be highly useful in guerilla warfare. *DR*

Many weapons enthusiasts took the 1940 model Smith & Wesson semi-automatic 9 mm caliber parabellum carbine for a submachine gun, as much for its shape, its magazine, and non-fixed breech. In reality, this weapon, devoid of its "automatic fire" function, is nothing more than a semi-automatic rifle. In spite of this, the British intended to use it as a weapon of guerilla warfare against the German invasion forces. *Dr. Maurice Brennett collection*

Photo extracted from the user's manual. *DR*

The most interesting arrangement of this carbine is its extremely long and wide magazine housing. The magazine is fully housed in the front part, and the rear section is empty and serves as an ejection port.

Two versions of this carbine were manufactured: the Mk.I and the Mk.II, bearing a cylindrical tube placed around the receiver and used to immobilize the bolt handle.

According to Roy G. Jinks, historian of the Smith & Wesson Company, 2,200 bodies were made, but only 1,227 complete carbines were assembled in 1940, only 200 of which were Mk.IIs. After the war, some of the surplus spare parts were used to assemble new carbines for the benefit of collectors.

Of the 1,227 carbines made in 1940, 1,010 were bought by the British weapons purchasing commission. Each one of the weapons came with two twenty-round magazines and a special key for the disassembly of the barrel. In the context of 1940, the British Army envisaged more purchases of Smith & Wesson carbines.

A contract was entered into between the purchasing commission and the manufacturer in which the crown promised to finance the tools necessary for manufacture on a greater scale. But this project petered out because the results of tests undertaken when the carbines arrived in Great Britain were catastrophic: the carbines tested displayed multiple firing incidents and breaking of spare parts. It is possible that the use of British made ammunition, much more powerfully charged than American ammunition,* may have greatly contributed to the poor results. In addition, the design of the magazine housing meant there was a risk of the case getting stuck and jamming the weapon.

Highly dissatisfied with their purchase, the British withdrew from the contract with Smith & Wesson and asked to be reimbursed for the sum advanced. Smith & Wesson, who were at that time going through a period of great financial difficulty, were incapable of reimbursing a penny. A friendly agreement was reached so as not to make the arms manufacturer bankrupt at a time when the free world was most in need of its products. The affair eventually resulted in the supply of Smith & Wesson revolvers to the British and Canadian Armies under preferential conditions.

The follow up to this affair came some years later when resistance fighters discovered Smith & Wesson revolvers chambered for the British .38/200 cartridge in containers dropped by the SOE.

After a very brief time in service (essentially, it would seem, in the Royal Navy**) the Smith & Wesson carbines, which had in the meantime proved their lack of reliability, were placed in reserve and replaced by Thompsons, Lanchesters, and Stens. After the war, the majority of them were destroyed, which simply made the remaining ones more valuable for collectors.

In 1974, during an inventory, a small batch of Smith & Wesson*** 1940 model carbines was discovered in the stockroom of the Smith & Wesson factory. The BATF granted them the status of "collectible," gathering together weapons of great rarity which could be collected with no formalities, making the prices of the carbines that had survived up to that time soar.

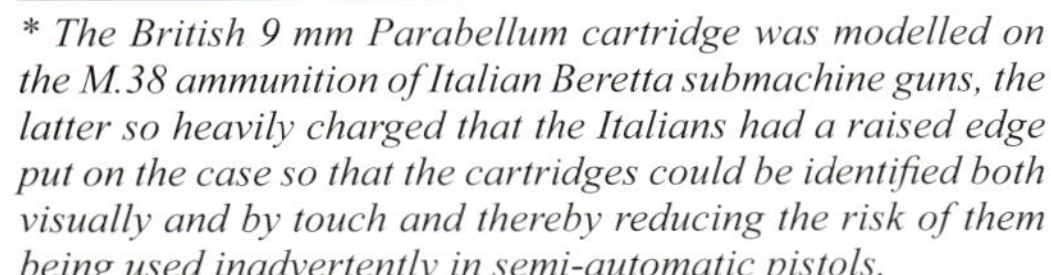

The British 9 mm Parabellum cartridge was modelled on the M.38 ammunition of Italian Beretta submachine guns, the latter so heavily charged that the Italians had a raised edge put on the case so that the cartridges could be identified both visually and by touch and thereby reducing the risk of them being used inadvertently in semi-automatic pistols.

*** The 1952 edition of the catalogue of handguns edited by the management of naval weapons mentions the 1940 model Smith & Wesson carbine. It can therefore be assumed that some of these carbines were part of the equipment of the French navy through the loan of British buildings to the Marine Nationale after the Liberation.*

**** To be precise, 217 weapons, made up of 137 Mk.I models and eighty Mk.II models according to Roy G. Jinks.*

This weapon has a heavy barrel, grooved in order to accelerate cooling: a method of manufacture out of step with the economic realities of war!

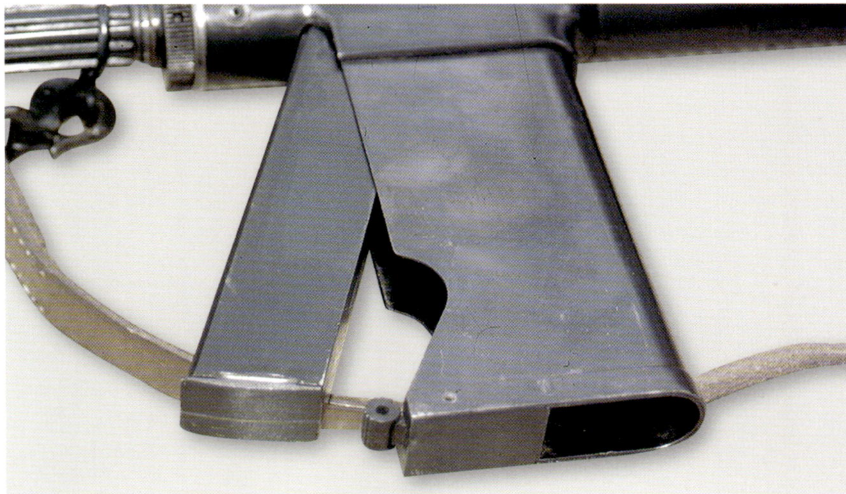

The unusual magazine housing of the 1940 model Smith & Wesson carbine has the magazine at the front and a long (and useless!) ejection pit for fired cases at the rear.

Smith & Wesson trademark.

Manufacturers marking surrounded by British proof stamps.

CHAPTER 1

BRITISH MADE SUBMACHINE GUNS

Marking on a Lanchester Mk.I. The letter 'A' after the serial number shows that the weapon is composed of non-interchangeable parts either for dimensional reasons or because they had been welded and were no longer removable. SA indicates it was made by the Sterling Armament Company. The letters were used before the alphanumerical codes designating the manufacturer came into force.

At the end of 1940, the British, seeing a large proportion of the US bought weapons destroyed in the German-led submarine war, decided it was urgent to make submachine guns on home soil.

There being no time for technical research, the simplest solution was to copy an existing weapon. The answer was the German MP28/11 submachine gun developed at the end of the twenties by the Haenel company from a design by the engineer Hugo Schmeisser.

The Lanchester: A British Schmeisser

This weapon, which had been exported or copied in many countries, was available in many areas of the world. It was Maj. Reginald Vernon Shepherd and the designer Harold John Turpin, both attached to the Royal Small Arms Factory at Enfield, who received the order to evaluate and set up production plans* for two copies of MP28/II** that the British Consul General in Addis-Ababa had managed to acquire and send to the light weapons inspection department team.

** The British machine tools were calibrated in the Imperial measurement system (also called Whitworth) so an adjustment of the weapons plans to metric was necessary.*

*** One a 7.63 mm caliber Mauser and the other a 9 mm Parabellum ; the British Army wisely opted for the second caliber, identical to those of Italian and German submachine guns, which later meant that resistance fighters armed with British submachine guns were able to use ammunition taken from the enemy if necessary.*

Marking of a Lanchester Mk.I. The magazine housing has lost its original anti-reflective, grey-green varnish. The M619 code indicates it was made in the Northampton factory of the Sterling Armaments Company.

British sailors armed with Lanchesters escort survivors of the sinking of the German pocket battleship *"Graf Spee."* They are blindfolded so as not to see the military harbor installations. *DR*

Lanchester Mk.I seen from the right side. The large key positioned at the rear of the receiver is visible. This locks the receiver and the bayonet lug in the frame for the fitting of the 1907 Lee-Enfield rifle bayonet.

Canadian combined operations commando, armed with a Lanchester, photographed during training. *DR*

It was necessary to make a weapon that did not need a complex manufacturing process. The machine tools and the workers capable of making them were, in effect, primarily reserved for the manufacture of Bren machine guns, of which only 2,300 remained in Great Britain in August 1940, from the 30,000 originally made, the remainder having been destroyed or abandoned during the Battle of France.

The War Department designated the Sterling Engineering Co. Ltd. of Dagenham, Essex, which before the war had produced electrical and radio equipment, to manufacture the British copy of the MP28/II.

The engineer, George Lanchester, a technical consultant to the Sterling company and an associate along with his two brothers in the car manufacturing company of the same name, had the task of organizing the manufacture of the weapon at Sterling.

After an order of 110 million 9 mm Parabellum cartridges was placed in the United States with the Western Cartridge Co., British industry started to make its own version: the "Cartridge Small Arms Ball 9 mm Mk.I Z," which was abandoned in September 1944, in favor of an improved ammunition "9 mm Mk.2Z," that is still in use today in the British Army.

George Lanchester brought several modifications to the MP28:

- The ejector was reinforced along with the blocking system on the receiver.
- The fire mode selector of the MP28/II was replaced by a switch positioned at the front of the trigger guard.
- The machined steel block, containing the magazine housing and the ejection port on the German weapon, was abandoned in favor of a part made from cast bronze. This design, also found on Spanish copies of the MP28/II, meant complex machining operations were saved by replacing them with a simple cast of an easy-flow metal, with sufficient resistance and in abundant supply in the subsurface of the United Kingdom.
- On the Lanchester, the butt of the MP28/II hand gun progressed to a butt based on that of the Lee-Enfield rifle and having a butt plate with a flap giving access to a housing where the cleaning kit (oil can, weighted string) could be stored.
- A bayonet lug, allowing the use of the 1907 model Lee-Enfield bayonet was added under the perforated protective barrel case.
- The foresight was protected by two solid lateral reinforcements.
- The magazine was modelled on that of the MP28 but, in order to equal out the capacity of the Thompson drum magazine, it was lengthened so as to hold fifty rounds.

Modified in these ways, this British MP28/II lost the compactness of its German model and was both unbalanced and ungainly.

The Lanchester submachine gun functioned according to the open bolt and non-fixed principle of firing with a firing pin independent of the breech and a large diameter recoil spring.

A series of tests of pre-production models, carried out in November 1940, confirmed that the calibration of this spring allowed the weapon to function with British and American made ammunition as well as German and Italian cartridges.

Mk.I sight made up of a simple bracket graduated for 100- and 22-yard distances, and solidly reinforced on either side.

Above: Mk.I Lanchester, and below a Mk.I* model.

A Royal Navy sailor with his Lanchester. ***IWM A 31 963***

During use, it emerged that its main weak point lay in its magazine, as it was a copy of the one on the MP28, in which the cartridges in a twin stack must line up into one as they approach the lips, a mechanism which rendered the magazine difficult to load and caused feeding incidents if the inner lining of the magazine was even slightly misshapen or if the interior of the magazine was not kept scrupulously clean.

Furthermore, the choice of a fifty-round capacity imposed an additional resistance to the movement of the cartridges towards the lips, due, in equal measure, to the increased weight of the column of cartridges that the elevator spring had to move, as to the increase in surface friction against the inner lining of the magazine.

Satisfied with these tests and under the pressure of time, the War Department adopted the weapon without delay under the name of Lanchester Machine Carbine Mk.I and ordered 50,000. In the course of its manufacture, the Lanchester underwent several modifications:

Very rapidly, the fire mode selector positioned in front of the grip would be removed, as it caused firing incidents. Thereafter the Lanchester only conserved one automatic firing capacity.

The backsight with leaf and slide screwed on the top of the receiver, soon deemed to be both unnecessary and costly, was replaced by an "L" shaped bracket with two sighting notches adjusted for 100- and 200-yard distances. This backsight was roughly welded to the receiver.

The hook-shaped bolt handle, deemed too long to manufacture and moreover having the problem of getting caught up in pieces of equipment, was replaced by a simple straight lever.

The version of the Lanchester Machine Carbine with an "L" shaped bracket and straight handle was called MkI*. At the end of production, a screw was added to the perforated disc positioned at the mouth of the barrel to prevent any accidental loosening of the screw, and some Lanchesters were equipped with a handle capable of blocking the bolt in a forward position to increase safety during transport of the weapon when accidental recoil of the bolt could result in loading and accidental firing.

Abandoned by the Army in favor of the Sten submachine gun, the Lanchester was finally assigned to units of the Royal Navy. We can see here a Lanchester Mk.I and a Mk.I* on a red ensign (flag of the Naval Reserve) along with an officer's cap, a Webley Mk.VI revolver and Barr & Stroud 7x50 naval binoculars. *Collection of the Royal Army Museum of Brussels and Le Poilu of Paris, Photo by Marc de Fromont*

An example of a piece rendered impossible to disassemble on this Lanchester Mk.I: the sight, initially screwed on the receiver has simply been welded which, from that point on, prohibits its disassembly and puts the weapon in the category of those identified with the suffix 'A' after the serial number.

"SECo" marking of the Sterling Engineering Company on a fifty-round magazine. Other magazines, manufactured by the Lines Bros. company are simply marked LB. The third manufacturer of Lanchester magazines was Accles & Pollock.

At the front of the trigger guard we can see the original position of the selector now closed after its removal.

Part of Winston Churchill's House of Commons speech of June 4, 1940, is engraved on the magazine housing of his Lanchester. *IWM FIR 62 6211*

Lever in open position, but can be cocked.

Lever in closed position, preventing cocking.

In order to speed up manufacture, Sterling called on approximately seventy sub-contractors to make certain parts of the weapon, and the final assembly took place on three sites:

- In the two factories in Dagenham (code S109) and Northampton (code M619) of the Sterling company, (58,990 weapons assembled having a serial number with no letter or preceded by the letter A).
- At the gunmaker Greener (code M94), (16,990 weapons with a serial number preceded by the letter G).
- At Boss & Co. (code S156) (3,900 weapons with a serial number preceded by the letter H). Making a total of 74,579 Lanchester submachine guns made.[***]

Despite the simplification brought to the MP28 by George Lanchester, and to the large-scale reliance on sub-contracting, the weapon was neither economical nor fast to manufacture. Fortunately for Great Britain and the free world, Reginald Shepherd and designer Harold Turpin, the two technicians initially in charge of laying out production plans for the Lanchester submachine gun based on the MP28/II, had the inspiration to propose to the British Army a weapon with the same operational principles as the MP28 and the Lanchester, but considerably quicker and more economical to manufacture:[****] the Sten submachine gun.

The adoption of the Sten in March 1941, led to the abandonment of the Lanchester, whose manufacture was stopped in October 1943. The majority of Lanchesters were issued to the Royal Navy, the combined weight and bulk of the weapon was however a less serious shortcoming on board warships than on an infantryman's shoulder. The Royal Navy was reasonably happy with the Lanchester considering the fact they were not reformed until 1978.

[***] The Guns of Dagenham, *by Peter Laidler and David Howroyd. Collector Grade Publications, 1995.*

[****] *In* The Guns of Dagenham, *Peter Laidler and David Howroyd mention that Sterling found it hard to deliver 3,410 Lanchester over twenty-eight months, while the BSA company delivered 47,000 Sten Mk.II per week!*

Lanchester Mk.I* identifiable by its straight-lined bolt handle and simplified sight. It has also been fitted with a safety lever enabling the bolt to be blocked in a forward position, not present on every Lanchester. Various accessories are placed in front of the weapon: a magazine pouch for three fifty-round magazines, a combined tool functioning as a screwdriver and a hook spanner to disassemble the barrel and a magazine loader which is kept in the pocket on the front of the pouch.

Marking on the inside of the magazine pouch.

The experience acquired in the area of weaponry with the manufacture of the Lanchester submachine gun encouraged Sterling to pursue research in the development of a simplified and lighter version.

This research culminated in, during the last months of the Second World War, the Patchett submachine gun, which will be presented at the end of this edition. The subsequent developments of the Pratchett would give rise to the Sterling submachine gun, one of the most successful post-war submachine guns, which would be adopted by the British army in 1956, under the name L2A3.

MINISTÈRE DE L'INTÉRIEUR

DIRECTION GÉNÉRALE
DE LA SURETÉ NATIONALE

" Section Armement "

NOTICE SOMMAIRE

SUR LE

Pistolet Mitrailleur "LANCHESTER" 9 m/m

N° P.M. 57808

Notice on the Lanchester 9 mm submachine gun edited by the weapons section of the French general direction on national security, intended for crews of river patrol boats who were equipped with Lanchesters after the Second World War.

Like its German model: the Schmeisser MP38/11, the Lanchester submachine gun is equipped with an independent bolt with firing pin and a large diameter recoil spring. *Michael Heidler*

A detachment of the Home Guard in the company of the group mascot. Both men in the foreground are armed with a Sten Mk.I. *DR*

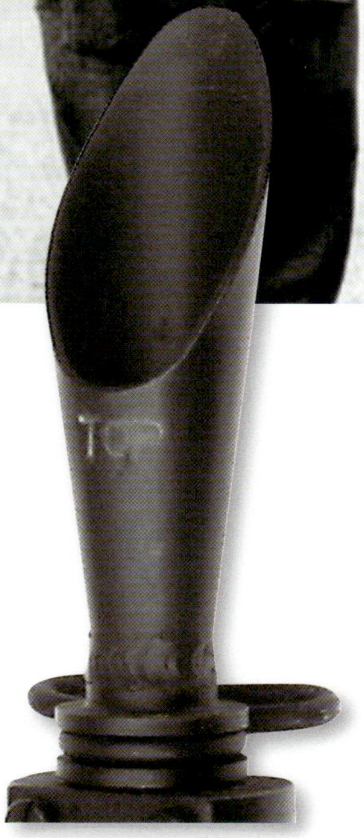

The Birth of the Sten: Models Mk.I and Mk.I*

As has been previously mentioned, the realization of the manufacture plans of the Lanchester submachine gun based on a German MP28/II and the transformation from metric to imperial measures was entrusted to two men with very great experience in weaponry: Maj. Gen. Reginald Shepherd, member of the design department of the Woolwich arsenal; and Harold Turpin, chief designer of the RSAF at Enfield.

Both men fulfilled the mission that had been entrusted to them with great swiftness and, fortunately for Great Britain and the free world, they didn't stop there.

Having come to terms with the fact that the British copy of the MP28/II, which was to become the Lanchester, was totally unsuited to large-scale, fast and economic manufacture, they started to imagine a submachine gun functioning on the same principle but conceived for mass production.

Their project was initially rejected by the War Department, which did not want to waste time developing a new model of weapon. However, the urgent need for massive quantities of submachine guns that the British army experienced at this time was to lead it to reconsider its position!

The weapons ordered from the USA were, for the most part, lost, because German U-boats sank large numbers of ships transporting them. In other respects these purchases, paid for in cash abroad, exhausted British Treasury funds. In short, it was proved that the Lanchester submachine gun that had just been put into manufacture was both slow and costly to make.

The project of an ultra-simplified submachine gun drawn up by Shepherd and Turpin from then on held the attention of the commission in charge of looking into the simplification of light weapons manufacture (created by the British army at the end of 1940). The commission asked the two inventors to present a prototype of their weapon as quickly as possible.

The conical and beveled flash-concealer is also conceived to act as a lift-up compensator and is marked "TOP" to avoid errors in positioning during reassembly. Because of its distinctive profile the manufacture of this part was time consuming and, as its usefulness was doubtful, it was discontinued on subsequent models.

The Sten Mk.I is very close to the prototype T40. It has kept several archaisms (wooden handguard, folding grip, flash-concealer etc.), but it has the seeds of an extremely simplified weapon, one which Great Britain would soon be able to produce on a very large scale to arm its troops and the resistance fighters of occupied Europe.

Seen with an Enfield Mk.II revolver, magazines, and a black-out lantern, this Sten Mk.I brings to mind the dark days that Great Britain went through during the summer of 1940, when there was a threat of German invasion and ceaseless bombing from the *Luftwaffe*. *Collection of the Royal Army Museum of Brussels and Le Poilu of Paris, Photo by Marc de Fromont*

Model type on the magazine housing.

This photo shows the safety catch pointing down, an original feature on Stens Mk.I and I*. The fire mode selector that is visible under the safety catch is made up of a simple transversal lever, which has an effect on the divider. Pushed from right to left it gives machine gun fire and left to right, single shot fire. The bolt can be seen equipped with the first type of bolt handle in the shape of a straight rod. *PB*

Serial number and the initials SMC (Singer Manufacturing Company) under the magazine housing of a Sten Mk.I.

Comparison between a Sten Mk.I (below) and a Mk.II model (top), whose safety pin is pointing up as on the majority of submachine guns derived from the Schmeisser MP/II.

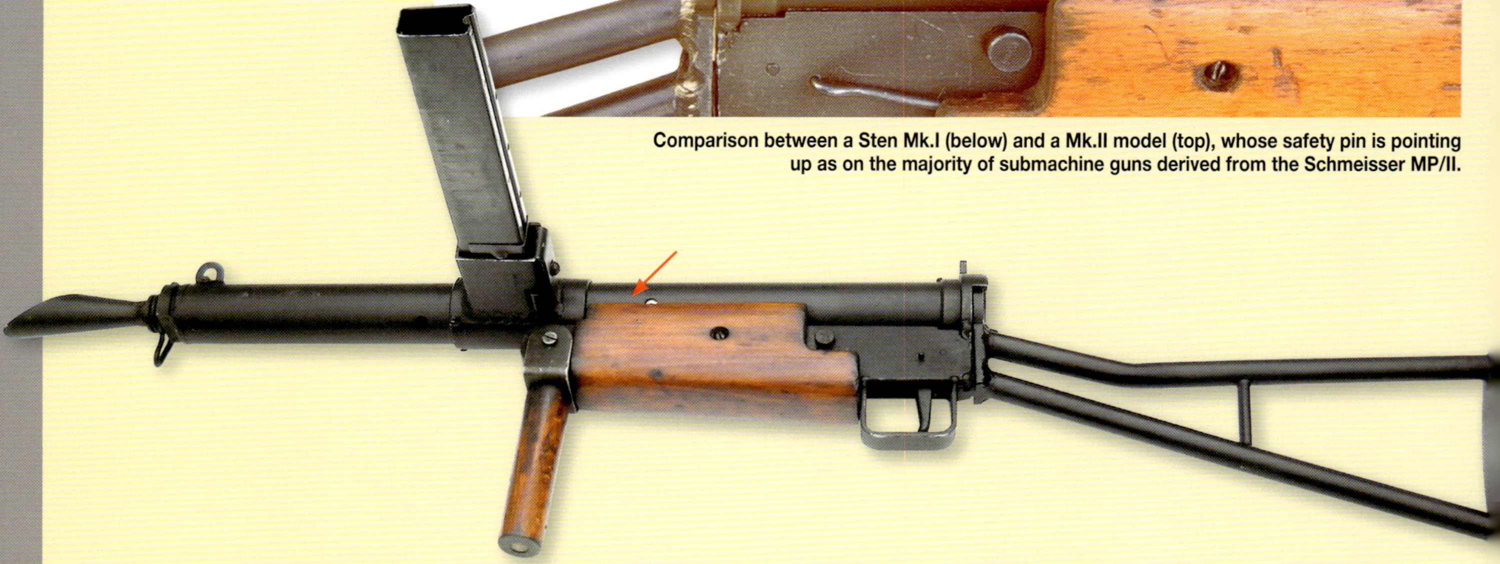

Sten Mk.I seen from the right. The magazine is interchangeable with that of a Lanchester, but its capacity has been reduced from fifty to thirty-two rounds, which makes it more reliable. The arrow indicates the orifice in which the end of the cocking handle is housed. The existence of this feature adopted at the end of the war, on a weapon of such an early production, resulted in a modification carried out when the weapon was reconditioned.

Above, front part of a Sten Mk.I*, on which the flash-concealer has been removed. Below, Sten Mk.I with its flash-concealer/lift up compensator. A wide sling ring for the assembly of the sling of the Enfield rifle. A narrower sling was to be developed for the Sten Mk.II and Mk.III but the rifle sling would be used for the Sten Mk.5.

Two prototypes, christened T40,[*] were made within thirty-six hours between December 1940, and the first days of January 1941, under the leadership of Maj. Hearn-Cooper, by the Philco Radio Works Company of Perivale, Middlesex. The first of the two prototypes was ready on January 8, 1941.

These weapons were made up of a majority of pressed metal parts, the manufacture of which could easily be sub-contracted out to small metal-works companies, of which there were many in Great Britain at that time.

The weapon was christened "STEN," made up of the initials of the surnames of its two designers (**S**hepherd and **T**urpin) and the first two letters of **EN**gland;[**] a name that was to become famous.

After rapid tests, the T40 revealed itself to be the submachine gun that Great Britain needed to arm not only her troops and those of the Empire but also armed resistance movements, which it was hoped would develop rapidly in enemy occupied territories. The new submachine gun was adopted on March 7, 1941, under the name "Carbine Machine Sten Mk.I."

Above, Mk.I model, below Mk.I* that ushered in the all-metal version of the Sten.

The Sten Mk.I

Mass production of the weapons was entrusted to a metal works near Glasgow in Scotland: the Singer manufacturing Company.[***] The relatively rapid manufacturing setup meant the first weapons were delivered to troops in October 1941.

The mass-produced weapon was very close to the T40 prototypes tested a few months earlier. It was made up of a cylindrical receiver, under which a housing for the trigger mechanism was welded. This was protected by a wooden handguard equipped with a folding foregrip.

The butt was not made of folded flat iron as on the prototypes, but two tubes with a flat butt plate welded at the rear. At the front the tubes were welded to the fixing part of the receiver. A cylindrical, vertical brace was soldered towards the middle of the butt, which reinforced its rigidity. This butt is known as "Butt No.2 Mk.I" under British nomenclature.

The gun sights were simply built of a fixed metal sight pierced for the eye piece and a conical foresight protected by two lateral braces.

A conical flash-concealer was mounted at the front of the barrel and beveled so as to act as a lift-up compensator.

The mobile breech was made up of a simple breechblock with a fixed firing pin (different from the Lanchester on which the firing pin was independent from the bolt).

The bolt handle slides in a side groove milled on the left hand side of the receiver. It has a safety pin positioned towards the bottom of the receiver. This unusual positioning originates from what had initially been planned; that the user operates the bolt with the right hand (as with a rifle) while the left hand held the receiver forward.[****] With this configuration it was more user-friendly to place the bolt handle safety catch towards the bottom.

[*] *The majority of details relative to the history of the Sten had been exhumed from British archives by Capt. Peter Laidler, former armaments officer in the British Army, who collated the information in a reference work entitled* The Sten Machine Carbine, *Collector Grade Publications, 2000.*

[**] *"England" and not "Enfield," as is commonly believed.*

[***] *The British government had to requisition the Singer factory for the war effort so as to lift the reticence that the management had concerning the production of war equipment. Singer was in fact a subsidiary of the famous American sewing machine manufacturer, that belonged to a nation that was still neutral at that time.*

[****] *This type of safety catch also exists on the German submachine guns MP18/I, MP28/II, EMP, MP38, and MP40, but also on others such as the French STA, the Swiss Sig 1920, the Austrian Steyr Solothurn, and of course the British Lanchester. On each of these weapons the safety catch is machined at the upper part of the bolt handle groove.*

Marking Sten Mk.I* on the top of the receiver of a Mk.I*. The markings on the lower part are identical to those on the Sten Mk.I.

Above: the Lanchester Mk.I, below: the Sten Mk.I*.

Several Sten Mk.I*s were among the weapons used in the film "The Guns of Navarone." The protected foresight on the weapon held by David Niven leaves no doubt as to its identity.

During use it became clear that the majority of users of the Sten tended to use the right hand to hold the weapon by the butt and the left hand for other operations (changing the magazine and operating the bolt handle). Consequently, on Sten models Mk.II and subsequent models the safety catch was positioned at the top of the groove, as was the case on the majority of other submachine guns.

The Sten Mk.I*

This variation of the Mk.I model resulted from three modifications designed to simplify manufacture:

- The replacement of the wooden casing by metal casing.
- Removal of the folding grip.
- The removal of the conical flash-concealer. This had proven to be of limited efficiency, both as a flash-concealer and as a lift-up compensator and whose manufacture was very time consuming.

The first contract for the manufacture of 100,000 Sten Mk.Is was passed between His Majesty's Government and Singer in March 1941. It was followed the next month by a new contract for the manufacture of a further 100,000 Sten Mk.I*s. A third contract for another 100,000 Sten Mk.I*s was concluded in October 1942. A remainder of parts meant an additional 149 weapons were assembled, that were also bought by the government.

Therefore, on the basis of these figures, the number of Mk.I made rose to 200,000 units and 100,149 for the Mk.I*. In spite of these high figures the Sten models Mk.I and Mk.I* are very rare on the collectors market.

If we assume that these manufacturing figures are correct, or at least near to the truth, then what has happened to those weapons? Were they withdrawn from service as a priority after the war and then destroyed, while later versions were kept in service? Or are they languishing under a pile of grease in a depot somewhere in the United Kingdom or in an arsenal in a Commonwealth country? The first of these hypotheses is, unfortunately, the most likely.

The Sten Mk.I and I* gave complete satisfaction to their users, but it still took twelve hours of work to make each weapon. The need to produce ever more weapons, more quickly and using as few raw materials as possible, led to the birth of a simplified version of the Mk.I* known as the "Mk.II."

Sten Mk.II with the first model of No.2 Mk.2 butt, widely christened "T" by collectors. The weapon is entirely made of steel. All parts requiring too much time to manufacture on previous models have either been removed (in particular the flash-concealer) or simplified. This effort to rationalize meant production would be faster and cheaper.

The Sten Mk.II

As a result of large quantities of this type of weapon being parachuted on to French soil to arm the resistance in 1943–44, the Sten Mk.II is without doubt one of the most well-known submachine guns in France.

This version has become today an essential element of the iconography of the Liberation, and it is difficult to imagine a prop master, for example, in charge of supplying equipment for a film set in this period, issuing anything other than weapons of this type!

French General de Lattre talking with an FFI officer armed with a Sten.

Presentation

The Mk.II version initially responded to a request from the Ministry of Defence dated March 24, 1941, to improve the compactness of the weapon in order to facilitate its use by airborne troops.

In his work *The Sten Machine Carbine*, Peter Laidler points out that Harold Turpin succeeded the amazing feat of presenting the first prototype of the parachutist Sten, which was to be later known as the Mk.II, a mere seven days after having received the directive to study the project from the authorities.

This close up of the rear of the barrel case allows the notch (A) in which the catch goes (B) to avoid any accidental loosening of the screw. By unscrewing the barrel nut without pulling back the catch, the rattling made by the pointy head of the catch against the notch could be heard. It is not recommended because of the risk of wear leading to premature unscrewing. This photo shows clearly the excellent finish on a Sten made in 1943, in Long Branch, Canada.

This version is distinct from the Mk.I* on the following points:

- Barrel easy to disassemble.
- Magazine housing could be turned 90° towards the bottom to reduce the dimension of the weapon in transport (this became a highly appreciable feature as it meant a maximum number of weapons could be put in paradrop containers).
- Bolt handle safety catch positioned at the top (and no longer at the bottom) of the cocking slot.

As has been mentioned in the first part of this article, the users of the Sten Mk.I and I* rapidly came to the conclusion that, rather than cocking the weapon with the right hand, it was more practical to hold the grip with the right hand and to pass the left hand over the receiver to grasp the bolt handle and retract it. Equally, in these circumstances, it became more logical to position the bolt handle safety catch towards the top; adoption of a new type of butt made of a single tube ending in a rudimentary butt plate. This type of butt was christened "Butt No.2 Mk.2."

The Sten could be quickly disassembled into several loads with a maximum length of 33 cm. This advantage was particularly interesting for both parachutists and resistance fighters, who often had to conceal their weapons. *DR*

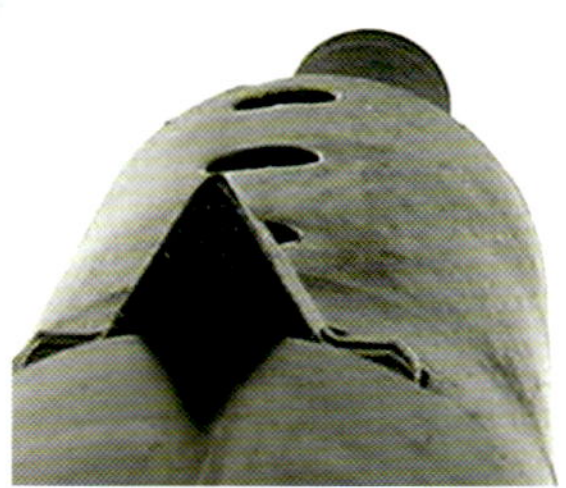

The foresight was slipped in a milled slot on the top of the receiver. It was then welded on after the adjustment of the weapon. Foresights of different heights (detectable by numbers stamped on the parts) allowed the height of the sight to be adjusted in the factory. The fact that the foresight was welded at the front of the receiver and the alignment of the eye piece/foresight was correctly positioned in the factory, the firing remained constant, even if disassembled, provided that care was taken to position the barrel correctly.

The barrel has a marker that must be consistently positioned in the axis of the line of fire during reassembly of the weapon, so as not to modify the point of impact.

Later, towards the end of 1941, another type of butt, the No.3,[1] made up of a U shaped metal bent in the shape of a rifle butt, was adopted as a replacement of the No.2 Mk.2.

In spite of its more elaborate aspect, the second type of butt was even faster and more economical to make than the first type. This model is generally called the "skeleton butt" by collectors, whereas the former model is called a "T butt."

The receivers on most British and Canadian Stens are made from a tube. Shortly after the beginning of the period of mass production of the Sten, there was a shortage of tubes.

To get around this supply shortage in such a critical period, the receivers on some Mk.II Stens were made with the help of an outline from press cut sheet metal, which was rolled around a spindle (these variations were known as "wrapped and rolled"). The two sides were then welded to the lower part of the receiver. Two extensions conserved at the rear section of the receiver were bent downwards to form the inner part of the trigger mechanism (whereas on weapons manufactured from tubes these parts were welded under the receiver).

When used, the receivers made this way proved to lack resistance. When the production of extruded tubes had once again reached a sufficient level, the manufacture of wrapped and rolled receivers was abandoned, and several months later, when the number of Sten in service allowed it, the "wrapped and rolled" were withdrawn from service and destroyed, making any surviving models highly desirable for collectors today.

The secondary components of the weapon also demonstrated minor developments during manufacture, which make these weapons particularly interesting to collect. For reasons of clarity, we have chosen to present these variations in a purely visual way as can be seen from the photographs in this chapter.

In addition to an increased compactness, the Sten Mk.II was comprised of only thirty-five parts, including the small screws, thereby proving itself to be considerably easier to manufacture than the Mk.I*.

The Finish

The Mk.I and Mk.I* models benefitted from a relatively decent finish. On the first Mk.II made in Great Britain, the welding was carried out in a very rough way. However, the finish on the Sten Mk.II improved steadily thereafter. The large, slightly trimmed weld beads assembling the arc-welded parts on the first Mk.II models gradually gave way to more thorough oxyacetylene welding.

For a while the Canadian arsenal at Long Branch abandoned production of four-groove barrels in favor of two-groove versions; quicker to manufacture and just as efficient. The finish on Canadian made Stens is more meticulous than on that of other productions.

Originally it seems that three types of metal protection were used for the Sten Mk.I, Mk.I*, and Mk.II:

- Semi-matt black bronzing, of the type used on British weapons before the Second World War.
- Grey satin bronzing.
- Coat of black paint.

Throughout their long career, which in some armies extended as far as the dawn of the seventies, many different finishes were applied on these weapons: parkerisation, olive green paint, grey matt paint of the Belgian army, or even camouflage paint.

---

[1] *This No.3 butt has three variations:*

1. An initial version, not widespread, equipped with a slanted vertical bar on its front part. According to author Peter Laidler, this brace was designed to attach the wide sling of the Lee-Enfield rifle, for which it had also been planned to fix sling swivel at the front of the barrel nut. Eventually, as a special type of sling was adopted for the Sten, the existence of the brace and the forward sling swivel were no longer justified and were thus abandoned.

2. The No.3 Mk.I stripped of the brace, which is the most common model.

3. The No.3 Mk.3, also without a brace, but having two clips in its lower part for the attachment of a cleaning rod.

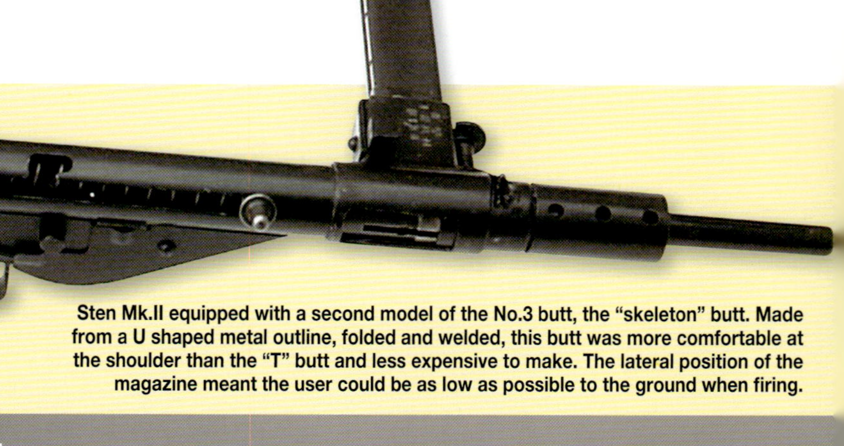

Sten Mk.II equipped with a second model of the No.3 butt, the "skeleton" butt. Made from a U shaped metal outline, folded and welded, this butt was more comfortable at the shoulder than the "T" butt and less expensive to make. The lateral position of the magazine meant the user could be as low as possible to the ground when firing.

From December 1942, Great Britain was not only fighting on the European and North African fronts, but also in the Far East when the Japanese attacked British possessions in the East and the Pacific. Japanese type 1 light machine gun, seen here with a Sten Mk.II, an Enfield Mk.II revolver (still with its hammer and double action lock) a regulation machete, beret, and Australian shoulder titles. *Collection of the Royal Army Museum of Brussels and Le Poilu of Paris, Photo by Marc de Fromont*

FIELD STRIPPING

Press the magazine catch and remove the magazine. This Sten gun belonged to a French resistance fighter who engraved a Cross of Lorraine and "Clairon" (bugle) on the magazine housing. This Sten is Canadian made and shows a rarely seen accessory: a fingerguard fixed on the barrel casing, preventing fingers from slipping in front of the ejection port.

Make sure not to point the gun in a dangerous direction. Cock the Sten, make sure there is no cartridge left in the chamber, ease the working part forward.

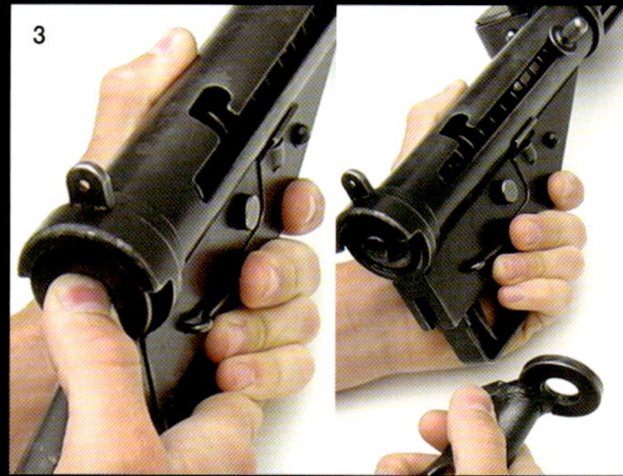

Butt. Press in the stud and the recoil spring housing and slide the butt downwards and off.

Bolt. Press the cap (or ring) round the stud inwards and turn it anti-clockwise; this will unlock it from its seating in the body.

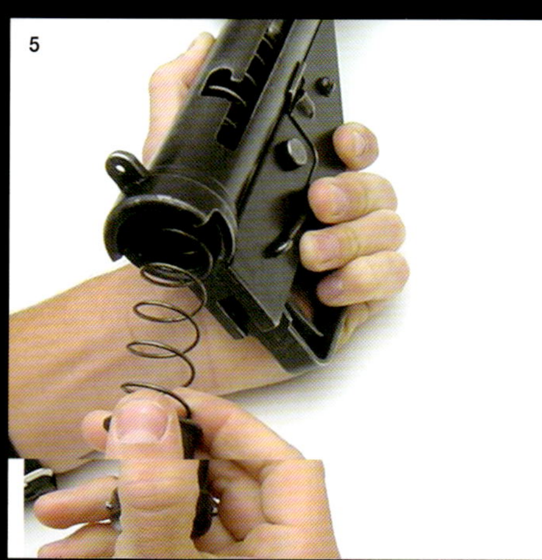

Remove the cap, spring housing, and spring.

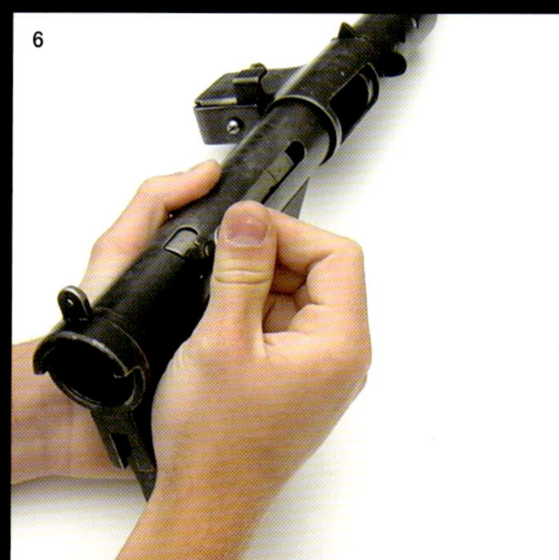

Draw the cocking handle to the rear, turn it halfway into the safety slot.

Remove the cocking handle.

Slide the bolt to the rear.

Remove the bolt from the body.

Barrel. Pull out the plunger on the side of the magazine housing and turn the housing downward.

Unscrew the barrel and barrel nut together and remove.

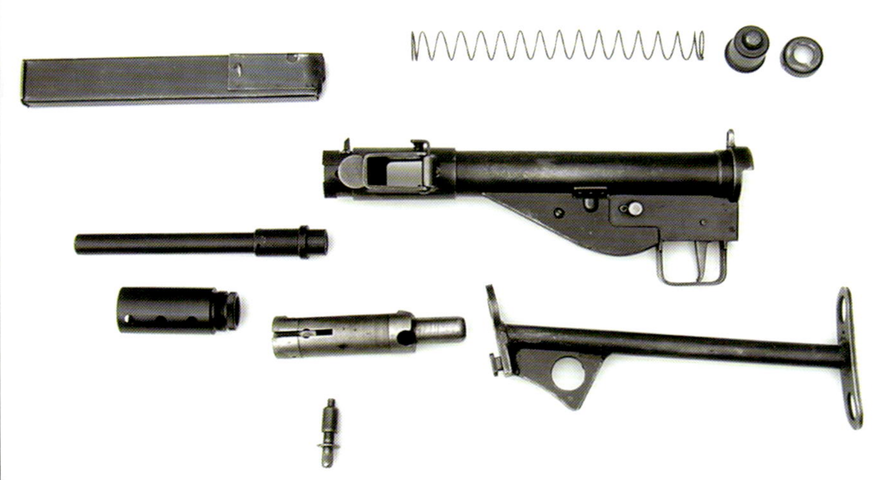

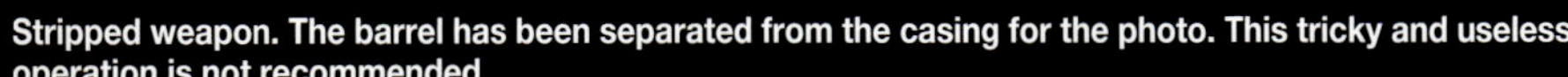

Stripped weapon. The barrel has been separated from the casing for the photo. This tricky and useless operation is not recommended.

The standard Mk.2 Sten barrel is a draw tube measuring 7.5 inches, rifled and chambered internally, having two or six grooves. The flanged sleeve is fitted over the rear end and retained by a pin. This sleeve pin also serves to retain the barrel nut by which the barrel is fixed to the breech casing.

During standard stripping the barrel and its casing stays together. There is a mark near the barrel muzzle (arrow) to help with putting it back in place correctly. By doing so it will not affect the gun sight adjustment made in the factory.

Switching the Magazine

Pull out the plunger on the side of the magazine housing and turn the housing downwards.

View of a Sten Mk.II with magazine turned downwards. This operation reduces the width of the gun, making it easier to conceal and providing protection against foreign objects entering the mechanism.

Holding the Weapon

Handling the Sten by the magazine does not offer a great deal of stability or compactness. It tends to favorize vibrations in the magazines, creating ammunition feeding problems. However, this position is certainly more photogenic. In this photo of Anthony Quinn in "The Guns of Navarone," the original barrel has been replaced by a blank-firing type. *DR*

Handling the Sten by its barrel casing, as recommended in the manual, offers a better control when firing in full auto. We notice that in this position the magazine lays on the forearm and does not affect the firing. *DR*

MANUFACTURE

Assembly of the Sten.

A view of the production line.

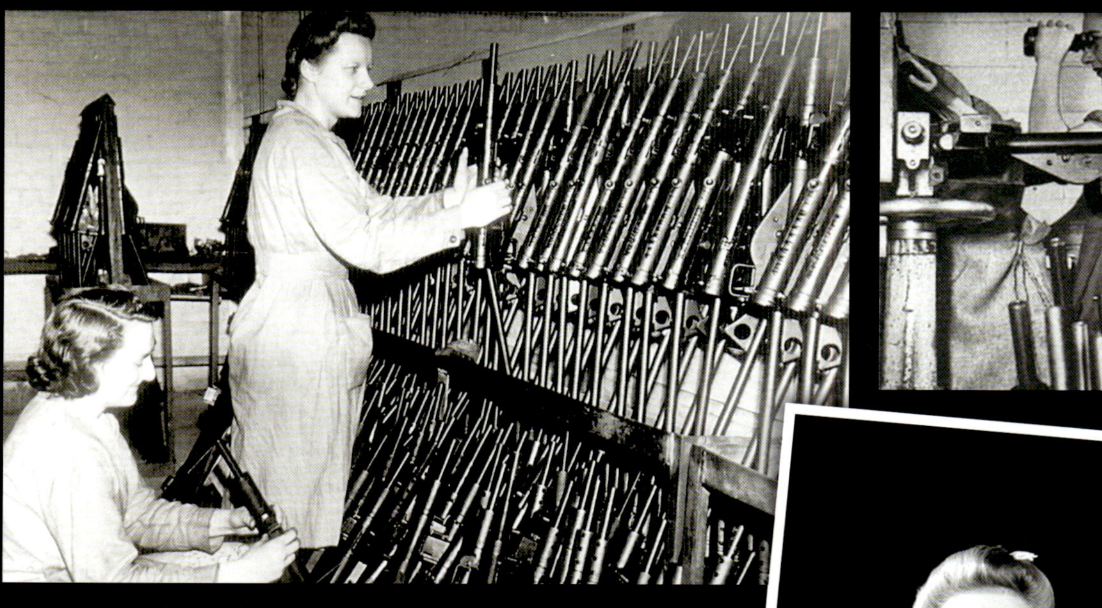

Adjustment.

Sten at the Tysley factory.

Checking the weapon.

Female workers.

Checking the finished weapons.

Training workers.

Welding a receiver.

Finishing the receivers.

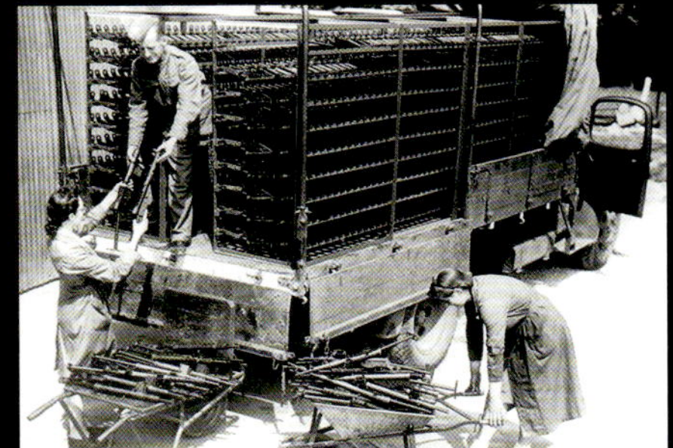

Loading up for transport.

Assembling the bolts.

Electrically engraved markings on a Sten Mk.II made by the Royal Ordnance Factory (ROF) at Fazakerley. These very light markings could easily wear away; the marking Mk.II has been re-stamped. The numbering, preceded by a code beginning with a letter "F" ("FD" here) is typical of this establishment; the faded markings were identically re-stamped when they became illegible, (in particular during the sanding process carried out before parkerisation when the weapon was reconditioned). In order to avoid confusion when original markings had totally disappeared, it became customary from 1950, for these weapons to be renumbered and bear a number preceded by the letters ZZ or SA55A.

Manufacturers and Sub-Contractors

Four factories made the weapon in Great Britain:

- The Royal Ordnance Factory at Fazakerley: an arsenal near Liverpool. Fazakerley-made weapons are identifiable by the letter F, sometimes combined with a second letter (FA, FB, etc.) in front of the serial number. On the first Sten made at Fazakerley, the number was electrically engraved at the top of the magazine housing. This marking, having the tendency to wear out through use, was often hand stamped on the upper or lower part of the magazine housing. Later, Fazakerley abandoned the electrically engraved markings in favor of traditional, pressed-stamped ones under the magazine housing.

- The Royal Ordnance factory at Theale, identifiable by the serial number preceded by the letter "T" or "TF."

- The Royal Ordnance factory at Enfield. The Stens assembled at Enfield are identifiable by their serial number preceded by the letter "E," "R," or "S."

- Birmingham Small Arms Company Ltd. (more commonly known under the abbreviation BSA). This private Birmingham firm, (the previous two manufacturers mentioned above were state-run arsenals), had to change the site of its Sten producing unit during the winter of 1941, to avoid German bombing raids. At the end of 1942, the production of Stens undertaken at the new BSA factory at Tysley in 1943, reached 25,000 weapons per month; it was to reach 42,000 per week! BSA-made weapons are identifiable by the letter "B" or the marking "BO" in front of the serial number.

These factories ensured the final assembly of the weapon and made some components. But the majority of Sten Mk.II parts were supplied by a large number of small factories. These sub-contractors marked the parts that they produced with a code made up of a letter ("N," "M," or "S"), followed by one to three figures. These letters indicated the geographical zone where the factory was located ("N" for North, "M" for Midlands, and "S" for South) and the figure identified the manufacturer. Some parts, however, did not follow this rule and clearly bear the initials or name of the maker.

In Canada, the Long Branch factory made Sten Mk.II for the Canadian and British forces, as well as for the Chinese army.

The Long Branch Sten bear the manufacturers mark and also the year of manufacture. The serial number is preceded by the letter "L," with a number from 0 to 13 in front.

In New Zealand, two firms made Stens: Precision Engineering Co. Ltd., and Radio Corporation of New Zealand (this production will be discussed in chapter 3).

Number on a Fazakerley-made Sten (always preceded by a letter code starting with "F": here "FF"). Deeply press-stamped on the magazine housing. ROF Fazakerley was the largest manufacturer of Sten in Great Britain during the Second World War. At the end of the war, this establishment also made Sten Mk.5 identifiable by the marking FY stamped on the trigger housing. In the aftermath of the war, it was given the task of reconditioning more than a million Enfield No.4 rifles, then manufacturing Sterling L2A3 Mk.4.

Sten made at Long Branch in 1943, bearing the traces of a mark made by a resistance fighter.

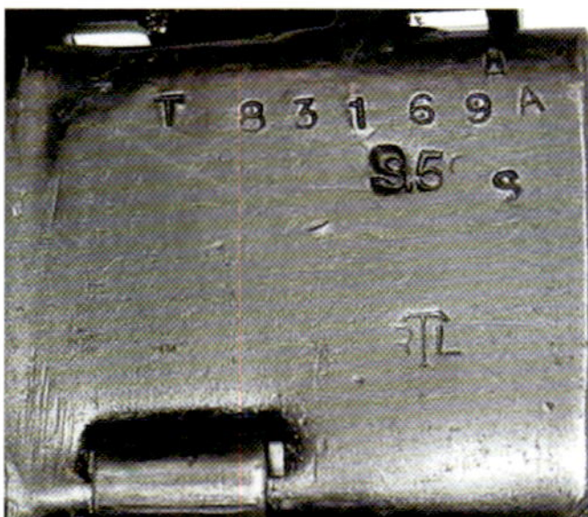

Initials RTL and serial number preceded by a letter "T," on a Sten made in Theale.

Marking of the Canadian factory at Long Branch.

Alphanumerical serial number on a Sten made in 1942, at Long Branch. Canadian Stens dated from 1942, corresponded to the very beginning of manufacture of these weapons in Canada. The "L" of Long Branch is here preceded by the figure "0"; this is one of the lowest serial numbers for this year of manufacture.

Theale-made marking. The serial numbers on Stens made at Theale began with a "T" in 1942 and 1943, then with "TF" in 1944. Theale went on to make the Sten Mk.5 identifiable by the marking RTL stamped on the magazine housing.

Serial number on a Long Branch 1943 Sten in which the "L" of Long Branch is here preceded by the number "4."

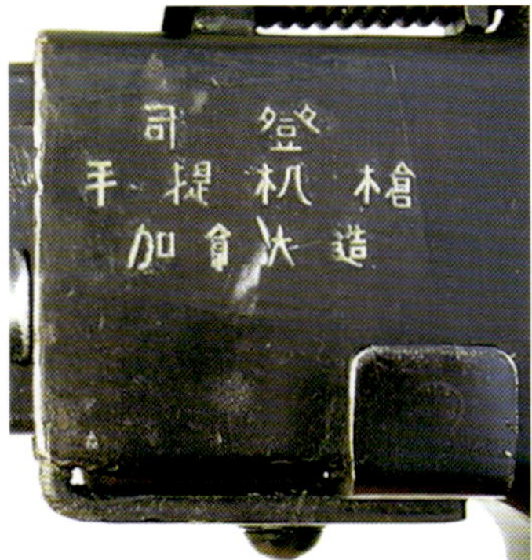

Marking on a Sten made in 1944, at Long Branch for the Chinese Nationalist government.

Serial number preceded by the letter "B" on a Birmingham made Sten.

Sten Mk.II assembly line.

Variation and Development of Parts

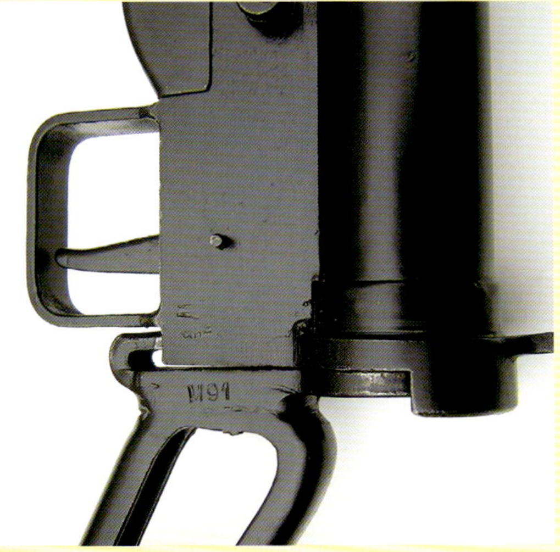

M91 marking on a "skeleton" butt identifying the manufacturer Godins Ltd. from Newport. The initial "M" indicates a factory situated in the middle of the country.

Body of a magazine marked N.93 indicating it was made by Kork-n-Seal of Sterling. The prefix "N" was allocated to sub-contractors based in the north of Great Britain.

Marking S106 of the firm J.W. Spears and sons of Enfield, Middlesex, on a trigger housing. The letter "S" indicates a factory located in the south of the country.

Initials of the company Elkington and Co., who made the majority of magazine housings for the Sten. Thereafter this firm used the code M78.

Two Canadian infantrymen from the *Regiment de Maisonneuve* positioned at the entrance of a German bunker protecting the banks of the Maas River (Holland), in January 1945. The cocking handle on the Sten on the left of the picture is locked in the safety catch as regulation dictates, except when the weapon has to be fired immediately. *DR*

Variations and Developments

A "wrapped and rolled" Sten, whose receiver is not made of a tube, like other models, but of a sheet of metal rolled round a spindle then welded. This Sten, representing the search for maximum economy, has a very basic finish: the welding is crude, the bronzing irregular, and the general assembly is rather rough. This example has an early version of the "skeleton" butt: the Butt No.3/Mk.0, with a slanted brace at the grip.

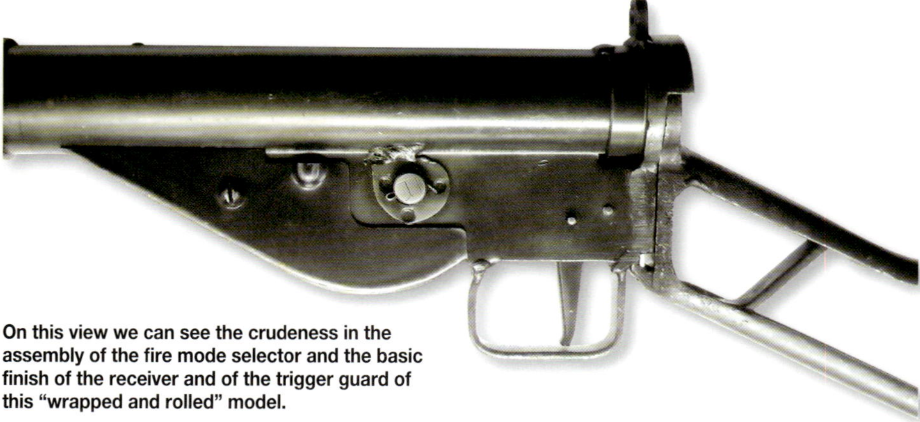

On this view we can see the crudeness in the assembly of the fire mode selector and the basic finish of the receiver and of the trigger guard of this "wrapped and rolled" model.

The arrow marks the zone where the two rolled edges join to form the receiver. At the top we can see the crude welding linking the magazine housing to the rotating barrel in which the ejection port is cut.

Development of the Parts

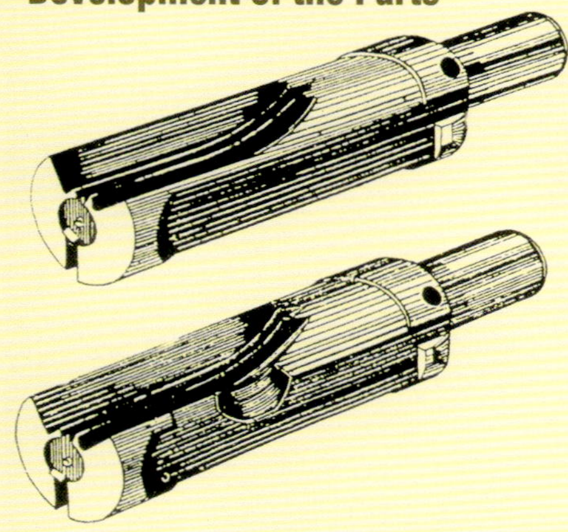

Unlike the Lanchester, the Sten is equipped with a fixed breechblock. The Mk.I bolt, initially supplied with the first Sten Mk.I, was rapidly abandoned in favor of the Mk.I* model, top, which was almost identical but has a cut out area to facilitate the movement of the separator.

To reduce production time, some bolts were made of cast bronze (unlike a lot of countries in continental Europe, Great Britain had an abundance of copper). *Victor Benson*

Two bolts Mk.I* and Mk.II. The Mk.II bolt, planned for the Sten Mk.5 has an indentation designed to adapt the trigger mechanism, as a result of its forward movement. The Mk.II bolt can also be mounted on Sten models Mk.I, I*, II, and III. For Stens with silencers there is also a lighter bolt named Mk.III. This bolt is presented in the chapter devoted to Sten Mk.II S.

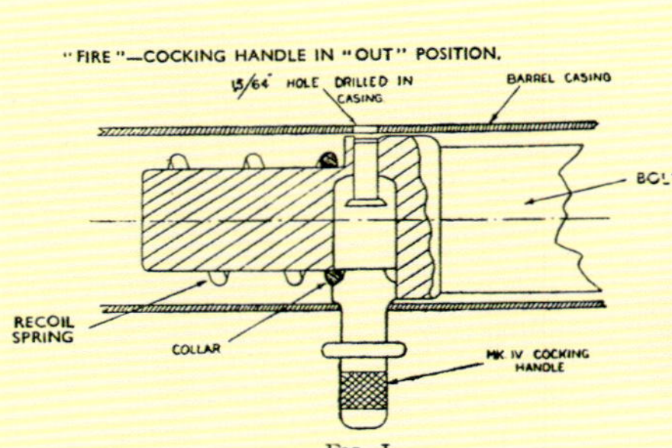

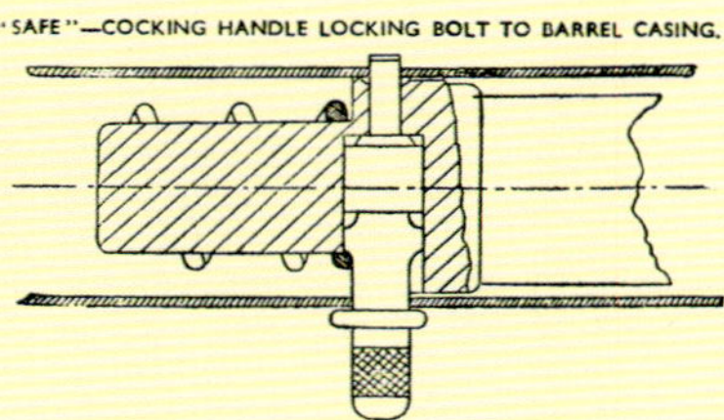

Diagrams showing the use of the cocking handle Mk.IV to lock the bolt. *DR*

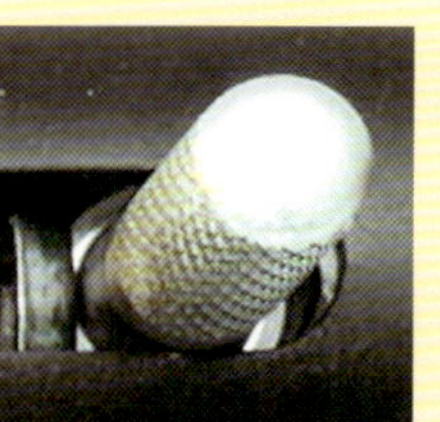

Mk.I cocking handle mounted on a Sten Mk.I and I*: a simple squared lever.

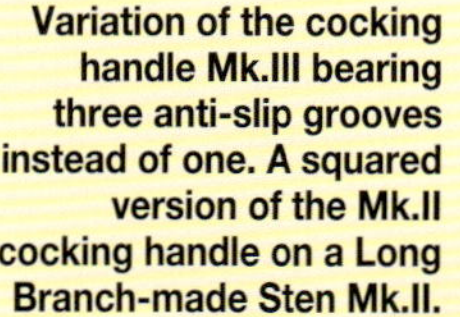

Variation of the cocking handle Mk.III bearing three anti-slip grooves instead of one. A squared version of the Mk.II cocking handle on a Long Branch-made Sten Mk.II.

The Mk.IV cocking handle was simply a Mk.II handle with a dowel at its lower end to block the bolt in a forward position by pushing the handle ("Push-in Safety"). When pushed in the bolt is locked in a forward position so as to prevent accidents caused by firing following accidental recoil of the bolt caused by an impact on the butt, or when the cocking handle gets caught up in bushes or undergrowth for example.

The Mk.IV model was rapidly replaced by the Mk.5 cocking handle, which gave a better grip for the user when pulling upwards.

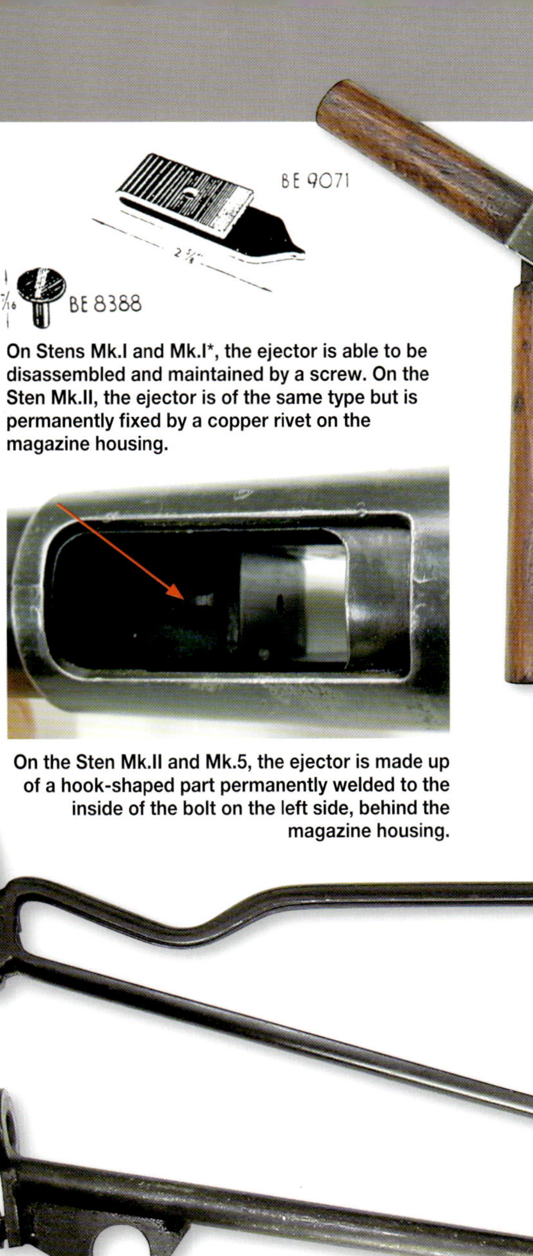

On Stens Mk.I and Mk.I*, the ejector is able to be disassembled and maintained by a screw. On the Sten Mk.II, the ejector is of the same type but is permanently fixed by a copper rivet on the magazine housing.

On the Sten Mk.II and Mk.5, the ejector is made up of a hook-shaped part permanently welded to the inside of the bolt on the left side, behind the magazine housing.

A B C

Development of trigger housings:
A. Sten Mk.I
B. Sten Mk.II
C. Sten Mk.5

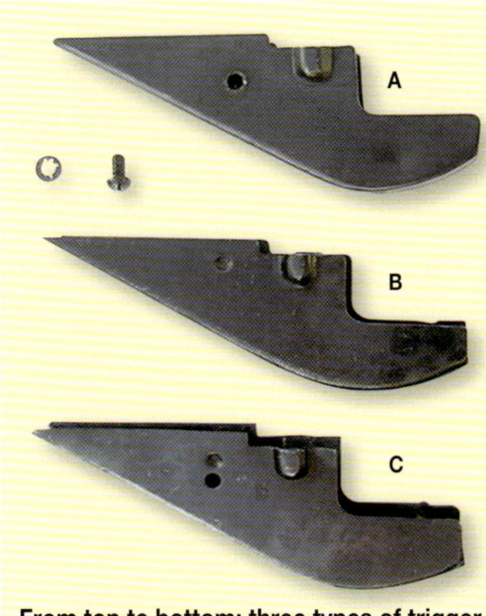

From top to bottom: three types of trigger mechanism housings:
A. Top Mk.I trigger housing for Sten Mk.I* and Mk.II
B. Mk.II housing fixed by a simple click and lock for the Sten Mk.III
C. Mixed housing which can be fixed from Sten models Mk.I* to Mk.III, either by screwing or by click and lock

There are two types of unlocking lever of the magazine:
- Mk.I model with added spring guide
- Mk.II model with guide obtained by cutting at the top of the push button and the cut flap is bent at 90°

The two different principles of the Sten Mk.II butt:
Top, the No.3 butt known as "skeleton" butt, and bottom, the Mk.2 butt, also called 'T' butt or tubular.

The Mk.5 cocking handle also allows the bolt to be blocked in a forward position by engaging the lower end of the cocking handle in an orifice pierced on the left of the receiver (arrow). The shape of the upper end of the handle facilitates it being held between the thumb and index finger when the user wants to release the safety lever. This modification brought a significant additional safety, post-war; many original handles were replaced by handles of this type whereas the receivers were pierced in a corresponding way. While the paradrop Stens are generally supplied with the handle of origin and present a non-pierced receiver, the majority of Stens used after the war by various armies possessed Mk.5 handles and had a pierced receiver.

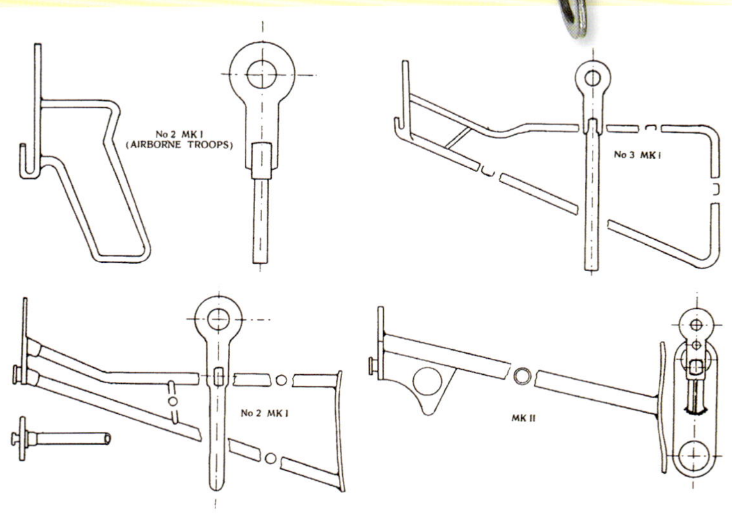

Different types of butt:
Top left: No.2 Mk.I pistol grip (Airborne Troops) mounted in the position of the butt.
Top right: No.3 Mk.I butt recognizable by the small slanted brace which reinforces the two parts.
Bottom left: No.2 Mk.I butt destined for the Sten Mk.I and I*.
Bottom right Mk.II butt. *Extract from Belgian Army manual, courtesy of Patrick Denamur*

For reasons of simplification some Canadian made Sten have a two-groove barrel (in the USA this measure of economy was also applied to some Springfield and Enfield No.4 rifles).

Accessories

"Filler Magazine Mk.I"; the Sten were delivered with a tool for loading magazines. An identical tool was used to load magazines on the Lanchester.

After placing the tool on the magazine, the loading handle is pushed to compress the platform.

While holding down the loading handle, a cartridge is introduced at the front of the magazine.

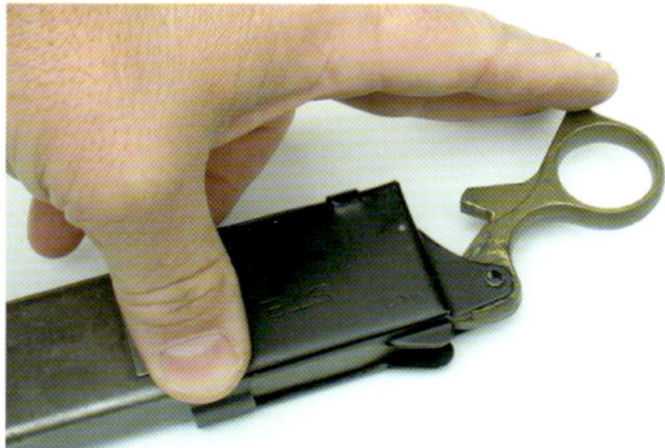

The loading handle is raised to push the cartridge down. The process is simply repeated to load a new cartridge.

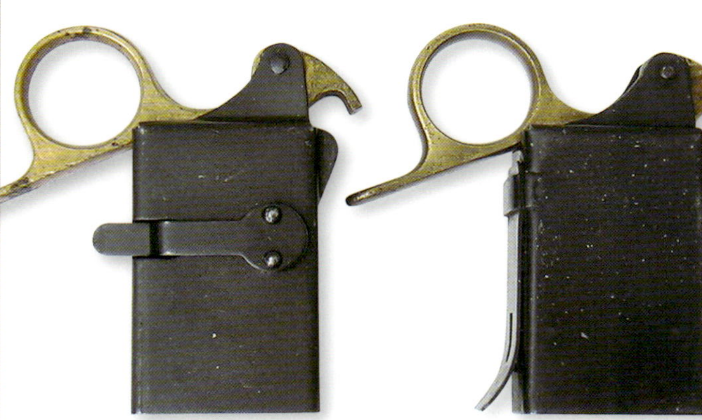

The first model of loading tool has two variations:
Mk.I (left), manufactured over a short period and therefore rare today, is locked laterally on the magazine.
Mk.II (right) much more common, which is locked at the rear of the magazine. In addition to the Crown property hallmark ("Broad Arrow"), these tools generally carry markings identifying the manufacturer. The tools made after the war for Stens of the Belgian army are marked "STEN" or "STEN Mk.II" in order to differentiate them from those made for the Vigneron submachine gun, very similar to, but not interchangeable with, those of the Sten, and marked VIGN.

The second model of loading tool, called the Mk.IV, is entirely made of steel and made of a single plate which is locked around the back of the magazine and loading lever at the top of the tool. This version, less bulky than the first, is also the most practical to use. It bears the manufacturers markings.

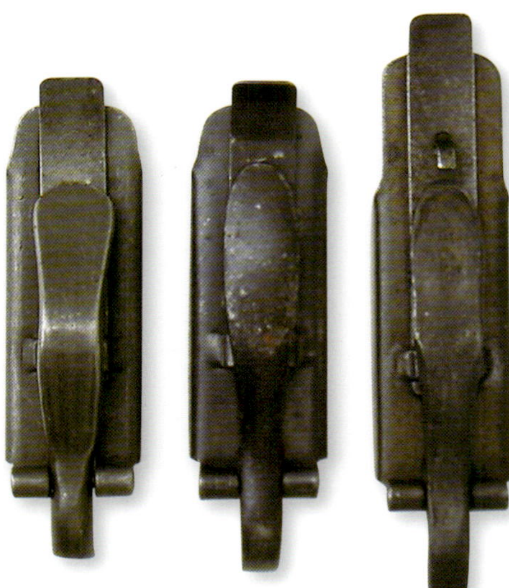

The dimensions of the Mk.IV tool can vary noticeably between manufacturers.

Some Sten have a small borehole (arrow) for fixing the fingerguard.

Fingerguard or Guard Ejection Opening: this useful, but uncommon, accessory is mounted by a clip on the barrel casing of a Sten Mk.II. It serves as a finger support for the user, and stops them from getting in the ejection port. On the Sten Mk.III a fingerguard of the same type would be welded permanently at the front of the ejection port. This safety element was to be forgotten on the Sten Mk.5 but then taken up again on the Sterling submachine gun.

Sten submachine guns were the principle weapon of resistance groups supported by the SOE. From left to right:

- **A container filled with explosives, time pencils.**
- **A Sten Mk.II S (with silencer)**
- **A Sten Mk.II (the most frequently parachuted model)**
- **A Sten Mk.III, several thousand of which were Para dropped during the last months of German occupation**
- **A "Gammon" grenade (which was very widely used by the resistance during ambushes and the protection of radio operators.)**

Collection of the Royal Army Museum of Brussels and Le Poilu of Paris, Photo by Marc de Fromont

Small metal tin for a Sten cleaning kit.

Contents of the tin.

When the cleaning string is out of its box, the manufacturer's code can be seen stenciled in white: M617, Illingsworth & Co. Ltd., of Mansfield.

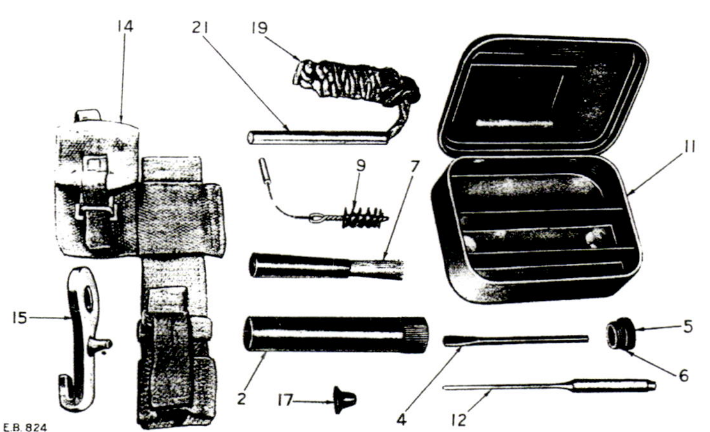

Cleaning tin and its accessories as they are presented in "List of Changes." This document also shows: a part allowing the use of the Sten Mk.5 without its butt (Ref 15) and a bayonet holder with a pouch for the loading tool, developed for the Sten Mk.5 (Ref 14).

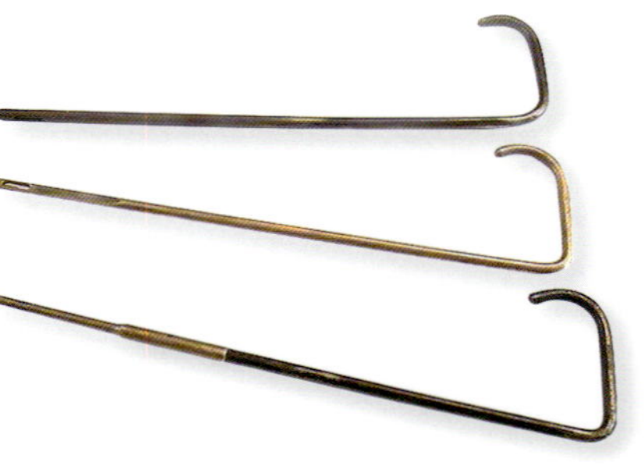

Cleaning rods with curved handgrip designed for the Mk.III butt. Examples in brass, steel, and steel with a brass tip. The Mk.III with integrated rods was relatively little used before 1945, but became more common in particular in the Belgian army.

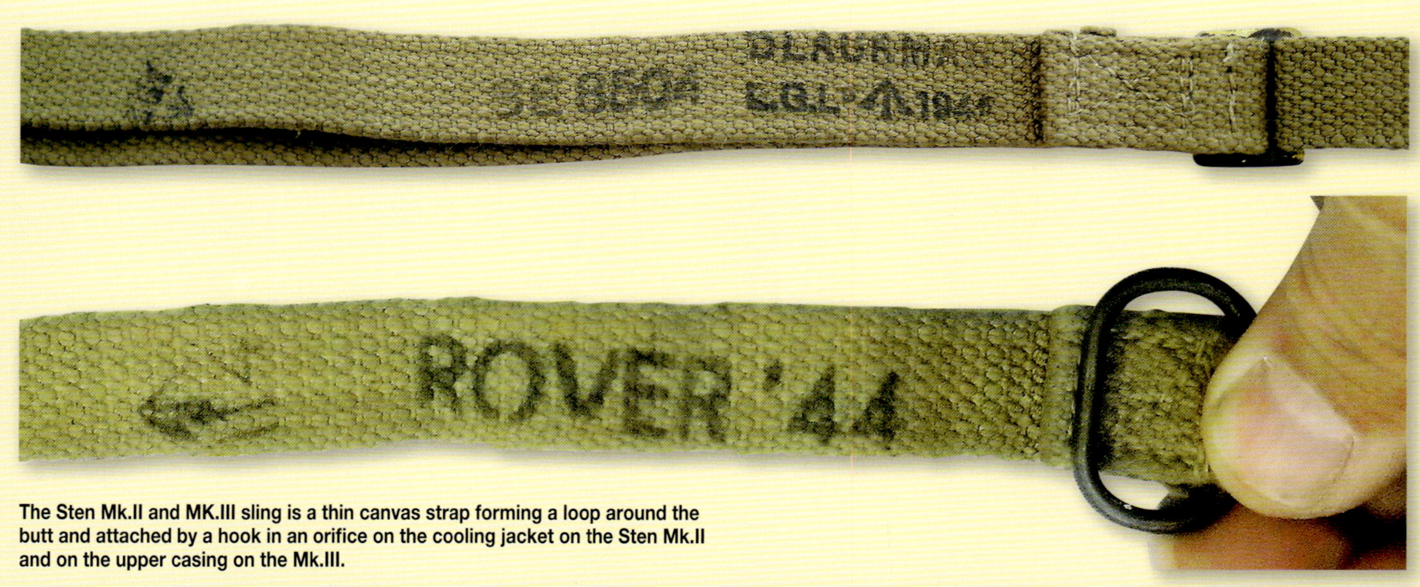

The Sten Mk.II and MK.III sling is a thin canvas strap forming a loop around the butt and attached by a hook in an orifice on the cooling jacket on the Sten Mk.II and on the upper casing on the Mk.III.

Canadian together with German sentries mounting guard at a control post at Ijmuiden, Holland, after the armistice of May 1945.

Two types of magazine pouches were used by the British during the Second World War: two three-magazine pouches were worn by every combatant armed with a Sten on the chest.

Pouch for seven magazines, designed to be worn across the chest. It seems that these models were mostly used by certain parachute units and also parachuted for the resistance. This equipment was made in khaki webbing or grey blue webbing for the RAF.

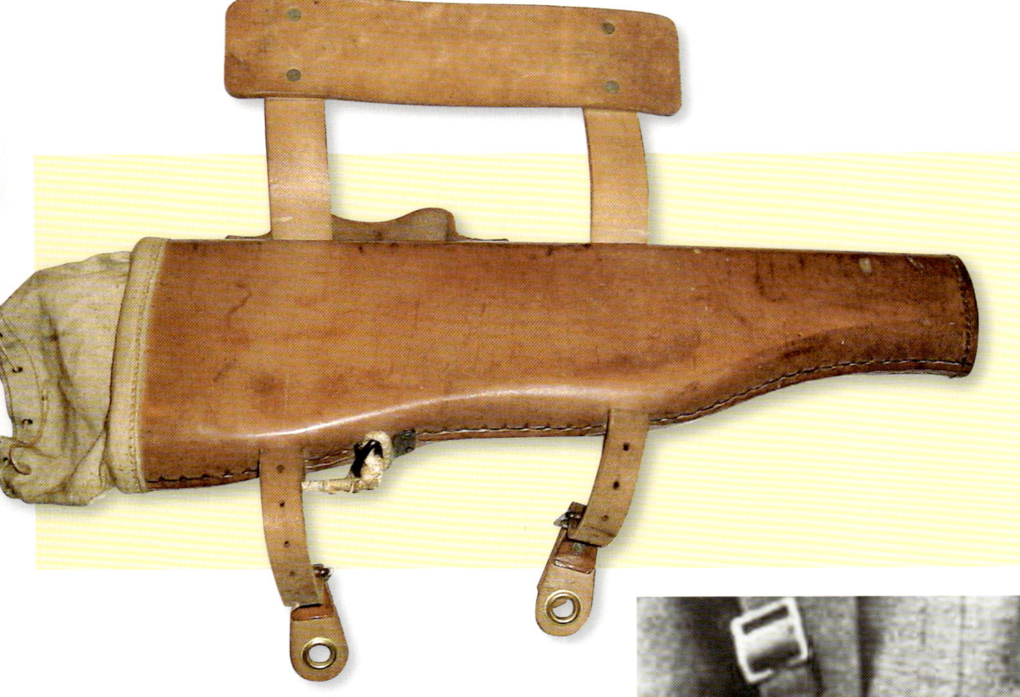

Case leg Sten gun made of leather. This accessory, destined for parachutists, was worn attached to the hip during jumps. Before landing, the wearer unfastened it and would leave it to hang underneath, in order not to be injured by the gun during landing. Only a small number of this luxury accessory was produced. Afterward, the paras jumped either with their disassembled weapon attached to their harness or with a canvas leg-bag containing the weapon and other equipment. *Michel Puntous collection, photo by Eric Puntous*

Bayonet with a tubular grip developed for the Sten Mk.II. The grip slipped around the barrel, and the spring placed above the grip supports the inside of the barrel casing. This bayonet was only produced in very small quantities but was produced in greater numbers after the war. The example shown in the photo is a reproduction.

Period photo showing another type of experimental bayonet that could be transported in the butt but was never mass-produced. *DR*

Magazines

Each Sten was delivered with an additional six or seven spare magazines. The production of Sten magazines during the Second World War is estimated at more than forty million. The magazines comprise a wide variety of manufacturing methods and markings, and we will give an overview here.

The body of the magazine was made in different ways depending on the manufacturer and the tools and materials available. Some come from the shaping of a seamless metal tube, whereas others are made from one or two rectangular pieces bent then welded to the forward or rear side of the magazine.

There are two main variations of the body of the magazine:

- The Mk.I model with four magazine viewing holes on the left rear side. It is worthy of note that some magazines, in addition, present two holes on the front side (which probably maintained the steel outline used to make the body of the magazine during folding and welding operations).
- The Mk.II model without magazine viewing holes.

The magazine bodies can be bronzed, painted in black, parkerised, or simply have a natural color which gives an appearance not dissimilar to that of some MP44 magazines, where the bare metal is simply protected from oxidation by immersion in an anti-rust product.

Many workshops, at least thirty, made magazine bodies and yet more makers supplied secondary parts to complete them (spring support plates, springs, and magazine followers).

The magazine follower was initially made up of a single U-shaped part. A support brace was rapidly added between the vertical branches. This part has a bronzed or stainless steel finish.

Apart from its weight and its bulkiness, the fifty-round magazine of the Lanchester submachine gun had the reputation of causing feeding incidents. So an identical model was adopted for the Sten, but with a theoretical capacity of thirty-two rounds (for optimal operation it was recommended to limit filling to twenty-eight rounds). However, the fifty round magazine of the Lanchester could be used on the Sten and the thirty-two round version of the Sten on a Lanchester.

Sten magazines produced in great quantity and with many types of both finish and manufacture. Seen here, from left to right: a parkerised magazine, a bronzed magazine and one made of a steel sheet bent and welded at the front.

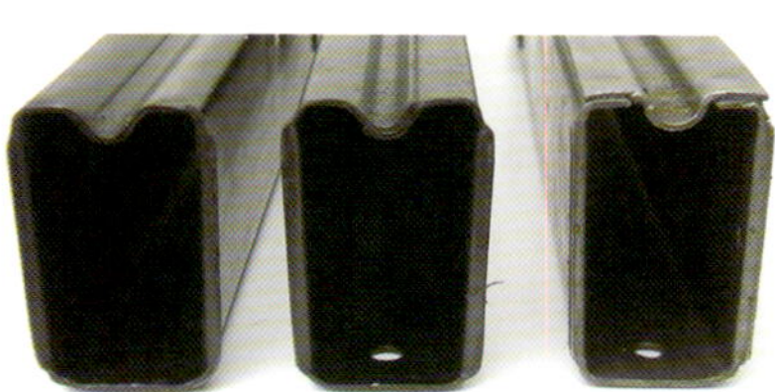

This photo shows three varieties of manufacture: the first on the left is made in an extruded tube, the second from a sheet of metal folded and welded at the level of the rear spine, the third is formed from two pieces welded at the rear.

The plate at the bottom of British magazines has an indication of the direction during disassembly.

In April 1945, a gunner of the Canadian Mont-Royal regiment re-loading the magazine of his submachine gun somewhere near Oldenberg in Germany. Having no tool to load the magazines, he has to push the cartridges firmly by hand and push the base against the ground. *Canadian Army*

Sten magazine with an SA proofmark showing it was used by the Finnish army after the war.

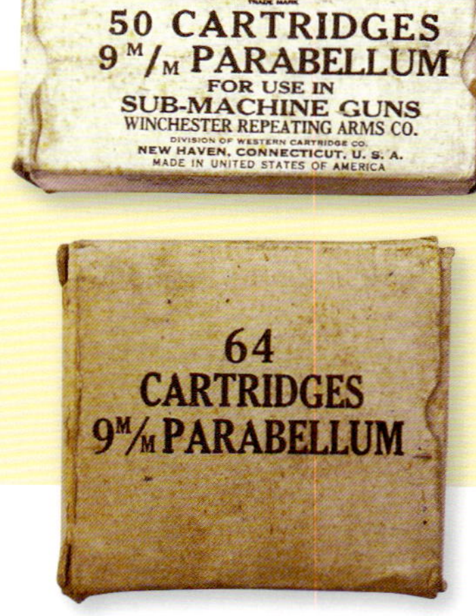

Two types of 9 mm Parabellum ammunition boxes, the most commonly parachuted into France; top, a box of fifty cartridges American made by Winchester, below, sixty-four British made cartridges (two magazines).

Magazine of reduced capacity of nineteen rounds made by the Indian army by the insertion of two guides in brass, forcing the cartridges to position themselves in a single row. These magazines, made in India by the Indian Central Railway Workshop (marking ICR1), were designed to prevent feeding incidents when the Sten was used in sandy environments. The arrows indicate the endpoints of the guides.

Photo of an instructional magazine, where the two brass guides can be seen. These guides, positioned on either side, reduced the friction of the cartridge column and stopped grains of sand and foreign bodies from interfering with the progress of the cartridges towards the magazine lips.

Sten Mk.IIS with silencer and a 7.65 mm caliber Welrod pistol silencer used by SOE agents during special operations. *Collection of the Royal Army Museum of Brussels and Le Poilu of Paris, Photo by Marc de Fromont*

THE RESISTANCE

Group of young resistance fighters in Montpellier.

A group of the FTP, enthusiastically welcoming the Americans in Chartres, brandishing Sten submachine guns. These weapons, for the most part, arrived by parachute and were an essential weapon for the resistance.

Front page of the journal "*Jeunesse Heroique*" (Heroic Youth), published at the Liberation, illustrating the school of the resistance, by Georges Sadoul.

Resistance fighters at Barbezière camp in Charente.

Group of resistant fighters and paras of a Jedburg team at the camp of Saint-Marcel (Morbihan), in June 1944.

Group of marksmen and partisans at La Mure-sur-Azergues in the Rhône Alpes.

Resistance fighters in Saint-Nicolas-du-Pelem (Côte d'Armor) posing for a photo, in September 1944.

A member of the FFI using a truck as cover from sniper fire near Dreux, on August 18, 1944.

Firefighters and American soldiers watching the parade from the roof of the Hotel Crillon, on August 29, 1944.

Sten Mk.II S. the lightened barrel can be seen in the opening of the ejection port. ***Collection of the Royal Army Museum of Brussels and Le Poilu of Paris, Photo by Marc de Fromont***

Close up of the silencer surrounded by its cover in thick canvas lined with asbestos, which protected the user from the heat given off during firing. ***Collection of the Royal Army Museum of Brussels and Le Poilu of Paris, Photo by Marc de Fromont***

The Silenced Stens

The development of a silent version of the Sten was carried out within two organizations: the SOE and the Royal Arsenals supplying the British army. The archives of the SOE were accidentally destroyed, and very little information is available on the Royal Arsenals due to the fact that the silent Sten was maintained in service until around 1972, and so information remained classified.

According to author Peter Laidler, their development was due to demand from active resistance movements in occupied countries. The first Stens Mk.II Ss ("S" for Special Purpose) were assembled at the Enfield arsenal, then an order for 5,776 Sten Mk.II Ss equipped with CEAD silencers was placed at the Theale and Fazakerley arsenals in February 1944. Several models of silencer were used. All of them operating by a combination of twelve rear and six front baffles situated inside the tube and held in place by a steel washer, which is retained by a hollow screw plug fitted with three packing pieces and an insulating washer.

These baffles, even though they reinforced the efficiency of the silencer, also had to be replaced regularly as their use led to a decrease of performance because of the passage of projectiles. Rapid fire was of course not advisable, and the SOE even put into service Stens equipped with a modified fire mode selector to make automatic fire impossible. The ammunition used was standard rounds but the presence of micro-perforations in the inner surface of the barrel was designed to decrease the gas pressure before the projectile entered the silencer itself. Some Sten Mk.II Ss were fitted with lighter bolts (called Mk.3 bolts) and shortened recoil springs, to ensure improved functioning. The heating up of the silencer during firing could make the weapon uncomfortable to hold, so the majority of silencers were fitted with thick canvas covers lined with asbestos fiber, inspired by those presented as heat insulators on Vickers machine gun radiators.

Another variation of the Sten silencer surrounded by its cover in thick canvas lined with asbestos. ***Collection of the Royal Army Museum of Brussels and Le Poilu of Paris, Photo by Marc de Fromont***

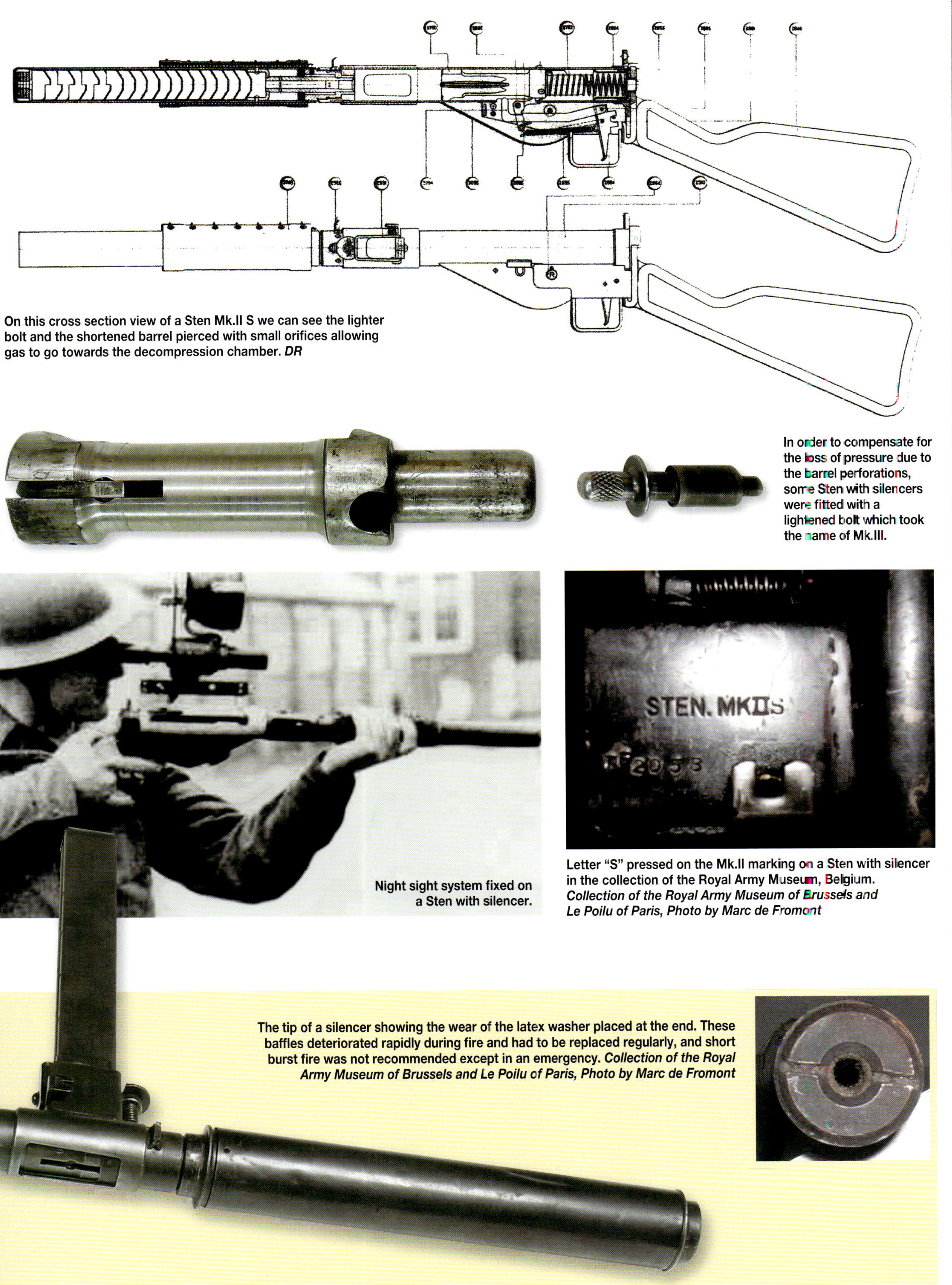

On this cross section view of a Sten Mk.II S we can see the lighter bolt and the shortened barrel pierced with small orifices allowing gas to go towards the decompression chamber. *DR*

In order to compensate for the loss of pressure due to the barrel perforations, some Sten with silencers were fitted with a lightened bolt which took the name of Mk.III.

Night sight system fixed on a Sten with silencer.

Letter "S" pressed on the Mk.II marking on a Sten with silencer in the collection of the Royal Army Museum, Belgium. *Collection of the Royal Army Museum of Brussels and Le Poilu of Paris, Photo by Marc de Fromont*

The tip of a silencer showing the wear of the latex washer placed at the end. These baffles deteriorated rapidly during fire and had to be replaced regularly, and short burst fire was not recommended except in an emergency. *Collection of the Royal Army Museum of Brussels and Le Poilu of Paris, Photo by Marc de Fromont*

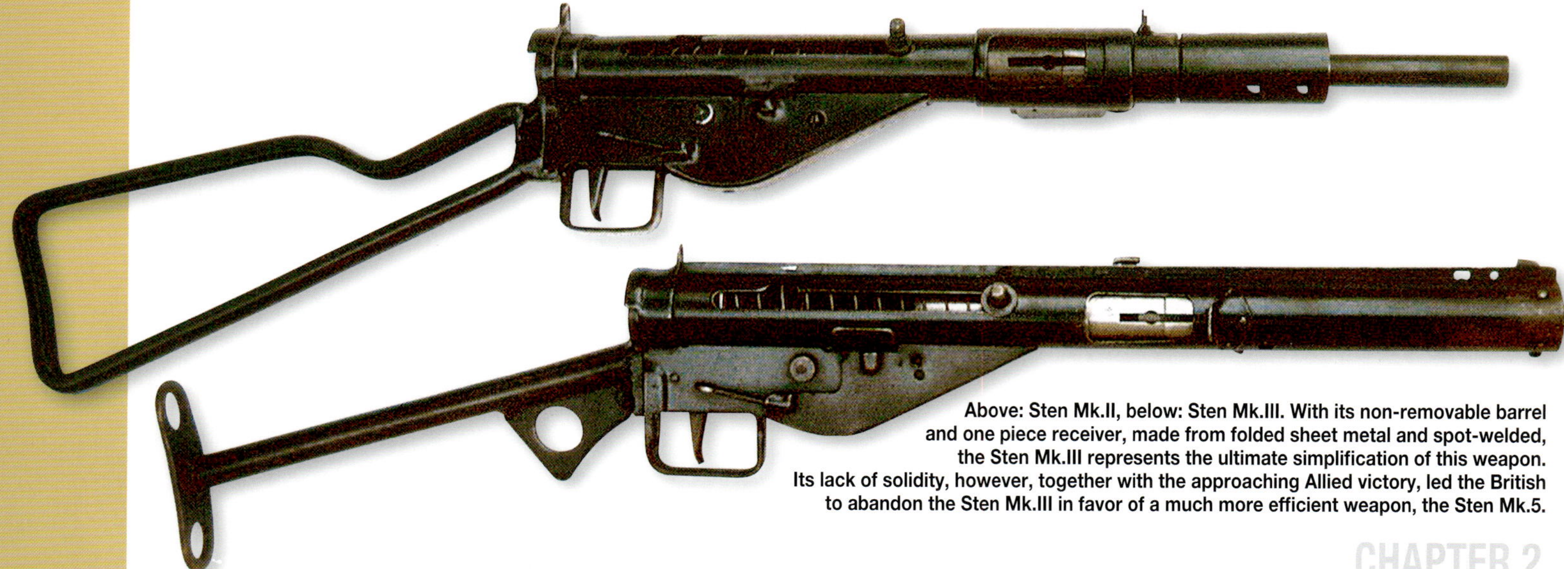

Above: Sten Mk.II, below: Sten Mk.III. With its non-removable barrel and one piece receiver, made from folded sheet metal and spot-welded, the Sten Mk.III represents the ultimate simplification of this weapon. Its lack of solidity, however, together with the approaching Allied victory, led the British to abandon the Sten Mk.III in favor of a much more efficient weapon, the Sten Mk.5.

CHAPTER 2

STEN MK.III SUBMACHINE GUNS

Marking on a Sten Mk.III magazine housing; Sten MC Mk.III. The initials "MC" stand for Machine Carbine, the official British name at this time for submachine guns.

A new milestone was reached in terms of simplification with the adoption of the Sten Mk.III, which was conceived by the engineers of a metal company: Lines Brothers Ltd., which had its factory at Merton, in the southwest suburbs of London.

Lines Bros., who already produced certain parts used in the manufacture of Enfield rifles and BREN light machine guns, had been contacted by the British government to make Sten Mk.I. The firm started by manufacturing some spare parts, while its engineers analyzed specimens of the Sten Mk.I submachine gun, and subsequently, after its putting into service, the Mk.II.

On the basis of their experience in the manufacture of parts in pressed steel, the members of Lines Bros. design department quickly became convinced that it would be possible to make a simplified version of the Mk.II using a maximum number of parts in bent or pressed sheet metal. And so the Sten Mk.III was born, and it represented the final simplification of a weapon that had already been simplified in the extreme since its creation.

The Sten Mk.III is a pared-down weapon. It is made up of a majority of pressed metal parts, welded or riveted. The barrel cannot be dismantled. The receiver takes up the shape of the Mk.I: a single cylinder, which surrounds the entire barrel except for the very last inches. Unlike receivers of the Mk.I and Mk.I*, which were made of a stretched tube, the Mk.III receivers are shaped from sheet metal rolled into a cylinder and welded in the upper part.

The full-length seam of both edges of the sheet forming the receiver linked the sight to the foresight. A bent metal sheet riveted at the front of the ejection port prevents the user from accidentally introducing the fingers of the left hand* and also bolstered the control of the weapon. The magazine housing is made up of a rectangle of folded sheet metal, welded to the receiver.

Inner side of a magazine housing marked "S68" identifying the Lines Bros. company. Other parts of the Mk.III bear simply the initials "LB." The serial number on the Mk.III is composed of a five figure number, preceded or not with a letter from A to H.

King Haakon VII of Norway, symbol of Norwegian resistance, examines a Sten Mk.III. The British officer in charge of presenting the weapon and doubtless with many years of strict respect of regulations behind him, does not appear to appreciate having the barrel pointed directly at him! *DR*

Sten Mk.III with a pair of ammo pouches with objects bringing to mind operations in North Africa. Colonial helmet and shoulder insignia of the 7th Armoured Division and the red gerboa that gave the men its name "The Desert Rats." *Collection of the Royal Army Museum of Brussels and Le Poilu of Paris, Photo by Marc de Fromont*

A fingerguard riveted on the receiver to block the users hand forward of the ejection port. It can be assumed that there were many injuries caused by fingers getting caught in the ejection port, justifying this precaution; a removable fingerguard was also commissioned for the Sten Mk.II, and this principle was kept on the post-war Sterling submachine gun.

Two folded flaps of metal used to hold the magazine housing, which is fixed by three welding points on each one of the flaps. The arrows indicate the rivets holding the rear ring in which the barrel chamber is fixed.

The receiver is made up of a sheet of rolled and welded iron. The assembly zone forms a very simplistic sight ending in a rudimentary foresight. The orifices seen at the rear of the foresight are used to fix the sling hook.

Canadian soldiers training. As one throws a grenade through the window the other prepares to spray the room with his Sten Mk.III. *DR*

Unlike that of the Mk.II model, the magazine housing on the Mk.III is fixed. The bolt, its recoil spring, and the trigger mechanism are identical to previous models. The trigger mechanism housing, if it conserves the shape of previous models, is kept in place by two hollows. The hole of the fixation screws nonetheless remains present on some Mk.III cases in order to allow their adaptation to the Mk.I and Mk.II Stens.

As on the Mk.I, the ejector is made up of the internal end (a triangular shape) of the rear reinforcement of the magazine housing. Both T-shaped and skeleton butts are seen on the Mk.III.

The presentation of the first prototypes to the Army technical services in late 1941, and early 1942, resulted in, after several minor modifications, a definitive model. 500,000 of these models were ordered in January 1942, and they were delivered in October of the same year.

If we consider the time needed to set up the production lines in a period when both raw materials and qualified labor were in very short supply, this was a remarkable feat and well illustrates the perfect adaptability of the Mk.III to the demands of mass production.

Line Brothers had developed its project so as to produce all, or almost all, of the parts for the construction of the Mk.III. This explains why almost only ever parts bearing the manufacturers code S.68 from this manufacturer are seen on the Mk.III.

The Sten Mk.III beat all records in terms of its speed of manufacture;[**] unfortunately, it turned out to be a lot less robust in the field than the Mk.II.

It had initially been planned to stop production of the Sten Mk.II in favor of the Sten Mk.III, but faced with the lack of sturdiness of the Mk.III, the order was given to suspend manufacture of the Mk.III and to pursue that of the Mk.II.

The majority of the Mk.III were allocated to the Home Guard. This territorial force, who ensured the safety of British territory, had, as seen in the first chapter, received Thompsons in 1940, with the aim of carrying out acts of resistance in the event of a German invasion of Great Britain. With this threat diminishing, the Thompsons were withdrawn from the Home Guard to equip commando units and troops in North Africa. The arrival of an abundance of Mk.III while the active army was already largely using the Mk.II meant the equipment of the territorial units could be brought up to standard.

The American-Irish William Joyce, before the war a member of Oswald Mosley's BUF (British Union of Fascists), sought refuge in Germany in 1939, so as not to be detained because of an article of law suspending habeas corpus (fundamental liberty of no imprisonment without trial). He gave himself to the service of Germany and made radio propaganda broadcasts for the benefit of the Reich. His broken nose gave him a nasal voice and led the British to give him the nickname of "Lord Haw-Haw." He is seen here lying on a stretcher after his capture by the British in north Germany at the end of the war. The soldier watching over him is holding a Sten Mk.III, highly typical at this period. William Joyce was condemned to death for treason and hanged on January 3, 1946.

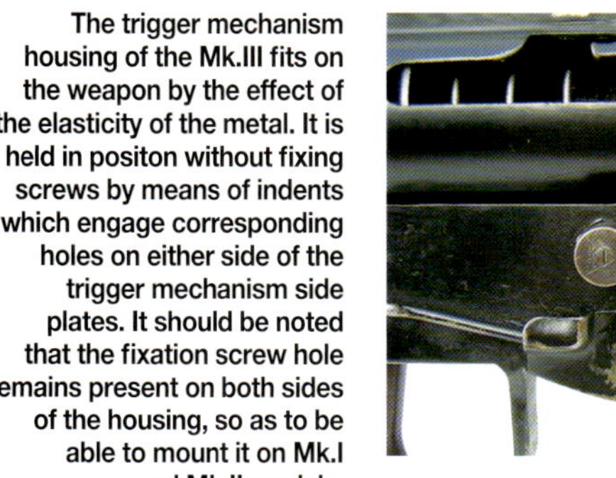

The trigger mechanism housing of the Mk.III fits on the weapon by the effect of the elasticity of the metal. It is held in positon without fixing screws by means of indents which engage corresponding holes on either side of the trigger mechanism side plates. It should be noted that the fixation screw hole remains present on both sides of the housing, so as to be able to mount it on Mk.I and Mk.II models.

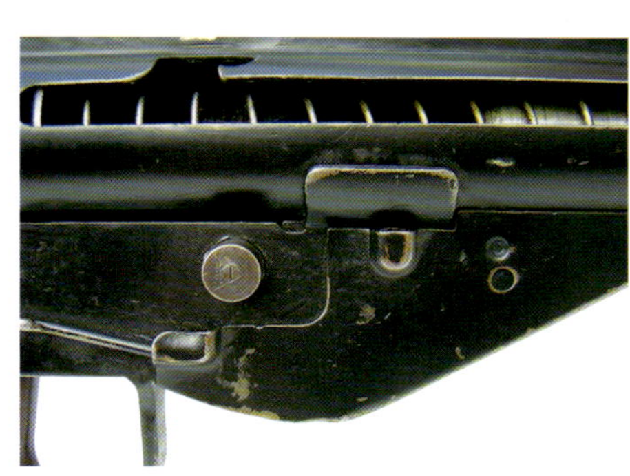

Group of Yugoslavian resistance fighters with Mauser carbines, ZB30 light machine guns, and some Sten Mk.III.

Sten Mk.III with a Mills grenade and a Gammon grenade, to the right a box of American made Winchester cartridges and a British made box of forty-eight British made cartridges, and a simplified tool for loading the magazines.

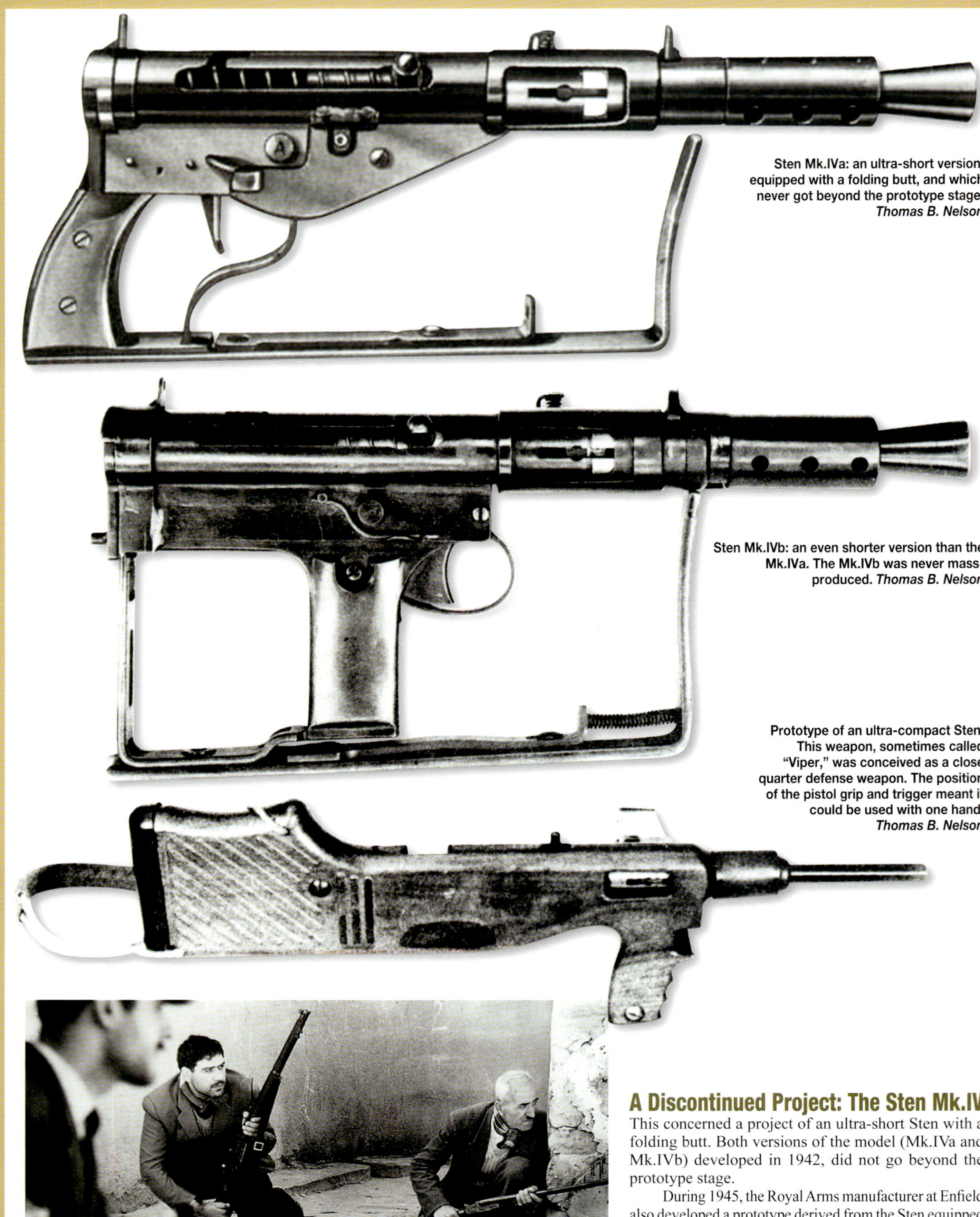

Sten Mk.IVa: an ultra-short version, equipped with a folding butt, and which never got beyond the prototype stage. *Thomas B. Nelson*

Sten Mk.IVb: an even shorter version than the Mk.IVa. The Mk.IVb was never mass-produced. *Thomas B. Nelson*

Prototype of an ultra-compact Sten. This weapon, sometimes called "Viper," was conceived as a close quarter defense weapon. The position of the pistol grip and trigger meant it could be used with one hand. *Thomas B. Nelson*

Sten Mk.III used in combat between Turkish and Greek communities in Cyprus after 1945.

A Discontinued Project: The Sten Mk.IV

This concerned a project of an ultra-short Sten with a folding butt. Both versions of the model (Mk.IVa and Mk.IVb) developed in 1942, did not go beyond the prototype stage.

During 1945, the Royal Arms manufacturer at Enfield also developed a prototype derived from the Sten equipped with a trigger mechanism and a forward pistol grip level with the magazine housing and a wooden casing surrounding the mechanism. This curious weapon, which had been conceived as a close-quarter defense weapon for military policemen or so a driver or motorcyclist could fire with one hand, was never mass-produced.

A sample of the excellent weaponry that British regular troops were equipped with, from left to right:

- A Mills No.5 fragmentation grenade: "Mills Bomb"
- Sten Mk.III submachine gun, cal. 9 mm parabellum
- Enfield rifle No.4, cal .303
- Bren Mk.I light machine gun, cal .303.

Collection of the Royal Army Museum of Brussels and Le Poilu of Paris, Photo by Marc de Fromont

Above: the Sten Mk.I, which inaugurated the Sten series. Below: the Sten Mk.5, which represented the culmination. The basic principles of operation are indentical, but the Mk.5 is ergonomically superior to its predecessor.

CHAPTER 3

THE STEN MK.V OR MK.5

The rear shoulder of the Sten Mk.5 barrel has a small recess (arrow) cut out of the locating flange, with a corresponding stud fixed within the barrel seating in the casing for an easy fitting in the receiver. In this manner its position remains constant in spite of disassembly.

At the end of December 1943, while the military situation in Great Britain was beginning to improve, a new model of Sten was on the drawing board.

After having imposed an increasing number of simplifications on the Sten submachine gun during the critical years, the British started to envisage commissioning an improved version of the Mk.II, with a more meticulous production, making for more accurate firing and more durability. The distinctive features of this weapon, which took the name of "Model Mk.V," were the following:

- a barrel able to be dismantled, as the model Mk.II, but fitted with a foresight block band, protected by two lateral apertures and a stud making it possible to fix a spike bayonet. These elements are of course inspired by the Enfield No.4 rifle.

- improved handling due to the adoption of a rear pistol grip, which imposed a shift towards the front of the trigger mechanism housing, which is slightly shorter than that on previous versions. It is a Sten Mk.II bolt, and the groove to house the trigger has been slightly lengthened.

- a barrel case fitted with two rows of six perforations between which is a band clamped round the barrel nut.

- the barrel is held in position by a stud connected to the body, which allows it to be systematically put back in the line of fire without the need for a sometimes inaccurate marker as on the Sten Mk.II. Every barrel was paired with a weapon; after the adjustment of the foresight, the weapon number was transferred on the base of the foresight to prevent any exchanges during disassembly. Also the number is transferred on the butt assembly plate as the butt is carefully adjusted to the body, suppressing the looseness of the butt stock as often seen on previous models.

The weapon entered into service in February 1944, under the name "Mk.5 Sten Machine Carbine."

The Mk.V was made from February 1944, to May 1945, by the two Royal arsenals at Theale and Fazakerley; the first arsenal produced 169,823 Sten Mk.V, the second 357,605.

The first examples of these weapons bear the marking "Sten Mk.V" on the magazine housing and later productions "Sten Mk.5," following on from the adoption of Arabic instead of Roman numerals in British nomenclature in November 1944.

The serial numbers of these weapons are preceded by a monogram composed of the letter "S" and "V" interlaced, it is supposed they represent the abbreviation Sten Mk.V.

Tip of a Sten Mk.5 barrel: the studs for locking the bayonet can be seen, and the foresight protector identical to that of the rifle No.4.

The Sten Mk.5 was fitted with a barrel, the end of which was similar to that of an Enfield No.4 rifle, which meant it could receive a spike bayonet.

Characteristics of Different Sten Models						
	Mk.I	Mk.I*	Mk.II	Mk.IIS	Mk.III	Mk.V
Total length (cm)	84.5	79.5	76	94	76	76
Barrel length (cm)	19.6	19.6	19.6	9.2	19.6	19.6
Empty weight (kg)	3.25	3.2	2.8	3.5	3	3.8
Length of manufacture	12 hrs				5 hrs 30 mins	
Manufacturers	Singer	Singer	Fazakerley, Theale, BSA, Enfield, Long Branch (Canada), Precision Enginee-ring, and LP (NZ)		Line Bros.	Fazakerley, Enfield
Quantity produced	200,000	100,149	1,950,000 by Fazakerley; 95,000 by Theale, 404,383 by BSA; 133,947 by Long Branch; 1,000 by Precision Engineering; and 10,000 by LP	5,776 by ROF Theale	876,794	400,000 by Faza-kerley; 126,719 by Theale (Mk.5 S, 24; Mk.6, 24,824)
Firing speed: around 500 to 600 rounds per minute depending on the condition of the recoil spring and the power of the cartridges used.						

This table collates information supplied in Peter Laidler's book, *The Sten Machine Carbine*. The reader can observe that around 4,300,000 Sten* submachine guns of all types were made, and 2,600,000 of those were Sten Mk.IIs.

** This puts the Sten submachine gun in second position in terms of the number made during the Second World War, behind that of the Soviet PPSh 41, the production of which is estimated at more than five million of the same model.*

The letters RTL can be identified on the magazine housing of the Theale-made MKV, whereas the Fazakerley-made ones bear the initials "F" or "FY" on the magazine housing or on the side of the trigger mechanism housing.

Unlike the previous models, the Mk.V was carefully made with only slight traces of machining remaining. The metal parts can undergo various finishes: bronzed, painted, or with phosphate then painted in black glossy paint.

The first butts were fitted with a bronze butt plate similar to those seen on many Enfield rifles. Just as on the rifles, this butt plate has a movable part allowing access to the oiler housing, made inside the butt. The latest models are simply equipped with a steel butt plate or have no oiler butt trap. Several other variations in the manufacture can be encountered in the construction of the foresight and its base and also in the strap swivel rings.

The Sten Mk.5 was originally delivered with a forward pistol grip which meant for an improved handling of the weapon during fire. This grip was held by a screw which holds the clamped band around the barrel nut.

With the Mk.I barrel nut used for the Sten Mk.II, the band came to obstruct the central row of three cooling holes situated in the middle part of the barrel nut. To get round this problem, a new model of barrel nut was adopted for the Mk.5: the Mk.II barrel nut bore two series of six round holes on the periphery of each one of its extremities. The support band of the forward pistol grip was fixed in place between the two rows of holes.

After 1945, the British army had a No.7 bayonet developed for men equipped with the Sten Mk.5. This bayonet has a rotating pommel at the rear of the grip, which means it can be used either as a bayonet on the Sten Mk.5 and No.4 rifles or as a dagger.

Corporals A. Burton and L. Barnett of the 6th Airborne, armed with Sten Mk.5s, survey a crossroads near Ranville (on the road to Caen), on June 7, 1944. ***DR***

Marking Sten Mk.V in Roman numerals above the serial number.

Sten Mk.5 marking with the "5" in Arabic numbers, above the M/78 code allocated at the end of the war to Elkington & Co. Ltd. of Birmingham, which specialized in the manufacture of Sten magazine housings. On this example the serial number is on the magazine housing.

A serial number preceded by an interlaced "S" and "V" visible under the magazine housing: probably signifying a Sten Mk.V.

"RTL" marking of a Sten Mk.5 made at the Theale arsenal. Weapons made at Fazakerley are marked with "F3" or "FY."

The Sten Mk.5 could be equipped with a No.4 rifle bayonet spike. After the war, the No.7 dagger-bayonet was developed, with a rotating pommel at the rear of the grip, which meant it could be used either as a dagger or as a bayonet.

No.7 bayonet with the pommel placed in the "bayonet" position.

Butt plates in bronze of the first made weapons and iron butt plates of later versions. Note that the sling ring is placed above the butt.

During production, the forward pistol grip was deemed to be too fragile. Moreover, it had been noticed that a lateral impact on the grip could cause the barrel to accidentally unscrew. The forward grip was therefore abandoned.

With the loss of the grip and its ring, the Mk.II barrel nut became redundant. The Mk.5 manufactured after the removal of the forward grip, were therefore simply mounted with Mk.I barrel nuts.

If logic dictated that early Sten Mk.5 fitted with Mk.II barrel nuts and forward pistol grip and later models have an Mk.I barrel nut but no forward grip, in reality all the various combinations of parts could be encountered.

As the Mk.I and II barrel nuts were interchangeable, they were exchanged in relation to the spare parts required. Some units did away with the forward grip, deemed an obstruction, of their own volition, keeping the original Mk.II barrel nut. Others, however, considered these grips to be practical for holding the weapon (particularly combatants using the Mk.5 without the butt) mounted either the Mk.I or Mk.II barrel nuts on forward grips taken from batches of stock.

Two versions of Sten Mk.5 silencer were developed; the first at Enfield was called "Mk.5 (S)" and only twenty or so were made; the second, developed at Theale, was known under the name of "Mk.6." The main obvious difference between these two resides in the fact that the Mk.5 is fitted with a ring-mounted foresight whereas the Mk.6 has a Sten Mk.II foresight welded as a permanent fixture on the receiver.

Sten Mk.5 submachine gun amongst objects of British Airborne troops: leg bag, toggle rope, beret, parachutist insignia, and helmet. *Collection of the Royal Army Museum of Brussels and Le Poilu of Paris, Photo by Marc de Fromont*

CHAPTER 4

A PROMISING PROTOTYPE: THE PATCHETT

British military policeman armed with a Patchett carrying out a road check in occupied Austria in 1945. *DR*

Marking on the magazine housing.

Marking used to position the screw locking the grip to its support: when the slot of the screw is in alignment with the letters FREE, it can be disassembled.

George W. Patchett, world speed motorcycle champion before the Second World War, had gained extensive experience in the area of light weapons through working at the Herstal firearms factory in Brno, Czechoslovakia. His knowledge was so valuable that he was exfiltrated from Czechoslovakia under the personal order of Winston Churchill just before the German invasion.

When he returned to Great Britain, he was taken on by the Sterling Engineering company, which at the time was organizing the production of the Lanchester submachine gun. As the weapon had been officially adopted, there was no question at this stage of modifying or improving it, but simply to make it as quickly as possible. Furthermore, its creator George Lanchester was not open to the idea of any modification of his work.

Three years later, the production of Lanchester submachine guns having been interrupted in favor of the Sten; the Sterling Company only handled the manufacture of various Sten spare parts, in particular the magazine housing.

Patchett, having considered the possibility of making better use of the Lanchester submachine gun by removing its cumbersome wooden frame and making it as light as possible, used various components of the Lanchester remaining in its factory to realize a prototype. This was how he succeeded in developing a compact submachine gun, equipped with a folding butt and a pistol grip positioned at the weapon's center of gravity. In August 1942, Patchett patented the fire mode selector mechanism of his weapon, activated by a simple lever with three positions cleverly placed in the upper part of the pistol

grip at the level of the user's thumb. The Sterling company detected interest and had several pre-production models made, which were presented to the British army, who tested them and ordered 100 for a trial within units. A number of these trial weapons were handed over to parachute or SAS units where they were so highly appreciated that some kept their Patchett when jumping into France or Holland, thus making the weapon a part of the last combats of the Second World War.

After the war, Patchett and the Sterling Company continued with the development of this interesting weapon, and the version named the L2A3 was adopted by the British army where it remained in service until 1994.

This Patchett, in the Royal Army Museum of Brussels, was used by Belgian SAS officer Lt. Paul Renkin when he was killed on December 31, 1944, at the age of twenty-five during an engagement with German troops at Bure in the Ardennes. Even though the Patchett was not yet regulation at the time in Great Britain, several examples given to the SAS to try out were used in combat in France, Belgium, and Holland. *DR*

Patchett delivered in 1944, to British airborne units.

In the last months of the war, British airborne troops, and in particular the SAS, started to be equipped with Browning pistols of the same 9 mm caliber as their submachine guns. The SAS also received at this time some new Patchett submachine guns. After the war, the British army kept the Browning as a regulation weapon, and in 1958, adopted a modernized version of the Patchett: the Sterling L2A3, the standard version of which can be seen on the left, and in the center the version with silencer. *Collection of the Royal Army Museum of Brussels and Le Poilu of Paris, Photo by Marc de Fromont*

CHAPTER 5

STEN COPIES MADE OUTSIDE GREAT BRITAIN

The R5 Gnome & Rhône submachine gun.

The French Sten: The Gnome & Rhône Submachine Gun

This weapon, for a long time unknown to the majority of collectors, was made by the Gnome & Rhône (G&R) factory in Limoges in the days after the liberation of the town. This firm, well known for its rotary piston engines for airplanes and motorcycles, had four factories; two in the Paris region (one in Gennevilliers , the other in Bd. Kellermann in Paris), one in Lyon, and one in Limoges. During the occupation, these factories were under the obligation to work for the occupying forces.

At the Liberation, this "forced economic collaboration" offered a pretext to the provisional government to nationalize. The arms industry was part of a general policy, begun prior to the war under the Front Populaire; with the objective of placing the arms industry under the direct administrative supervision of the State. Orders for various equipment were placed with recently nationalized factories before the end of hostilities, so as to enable them to get back to their activity rapidly and to keep the know-how of the personnel.

The cap covering the rear of the Gnome & Rhône submachine gun recoil spring.

The cap having a locking piece independent of the Sten submachine gun.

This photo of Gen. Monsabert, taken in Germany in 1945, shows his driver armed with a Gnome & Rhône R5 submachine gun clearly identifiable by its very short barrel casing. *ECPAD*

Close up of the receiver, showing the markings of the fire mode selector and the phosphate finish in grey-green, very similar in appearance to the parkerization carried out by the Germans at the end of the war.

It was in this context that the Limoges factory received an order for Sten type submachine guns destined for French combat units and to troops from the Resistance, which were struggling to reduce pockets still defended by German troops around the Atlantic ports (Royan, La Rochelle, Saint Nazaire, and Lorient).

In his book, *R5 au Coeur de la France, un champ de bataille secret où tombèrent dix mille Allemands*, Gen.Joinville mentioned an order of 20,000 type R5 submachine guns from the G&R factory. If we relate to this number the 8,000 collections of parts (butt and forward grip units) ordered by G&R from the subcontractor MAT, it is likely that the total number of G&R Sten manufactured was more in the region of 7,000 to 7,500.*

It seems that this order resulted from a local initiative of the chief of staff of the fifth military region of the resistance (R5), which constituted the south west of France. The situation in this part of France, which was liberated by its own means without waiting for Allied troops, was very particular, as the authority of the State was not completely re-established and the region continued to be administered by resistance authorities for several months. Within these bodies the communist resistance (FTPF) of Col. Guingouin exerted a dominating influence.

The motivation of this local manufacture is probably due to the fact that the Allies, just like the provisional government of the French republic, demonstrated a reticence to carry out new weapons deliveries to forces controlled by the communists, when the major part of French territory was liberated.

** To this order must be added the order of 100 R5 submachine guns passed in November 1945, by the DGER (Direction General for Research and Development): the French special services of the period.*

Close up of a movable part to immobilize the cocking handle in a forward position. This part had a tendency to rattle and so was often removed by combatants.

Left: long barrel casing on a Sten Mk.II.
Right: short barrel casing of a Gnome & Rhône.

This view shows the short barrel casing and the conical shaped foresight.

Left view of the Gnome & Rhône R5.

The setting up of a local production of a French copy of the Sten meant the chief of staff of the fifth military region could free itself from outside deliveries and establish the beginnings of an arms industry under direct orders in the event of the communist maquis trying to conserve power in the region.

The setting up of this production was carried out in a rather empirical manner: a worker in the G&R de Limoges factory, a former Franc-Tireur partisan, put his own Sten Mk.II at the disposal of the draughtsman, who noted the dimensions and set out plans. These plans, still kept today in the Châtellarault armament archives, shows a weapon that was absolutely identical to the British model.

However, the weapon which was made by G&R presents some notable differences with the Sten:

- wooden butt
- wooden pistol grip screwed under the magazine housing
- short barrel nut with just a single row of holes
- slimmer and higher foresight compared to the Sten
- mobile flap, positioned on the receiver, intended to block the bolt handle in a forward position
- the length of the barrel is increased by 6 cm (245 mm instead of 185 mm for the original model), in order to increase the accuracy of the weapon when fired in single shots

Finally, the receiver, along with many other elements such as the spring housing closing the rear of the receiver, are machined and not cut or pressed. This longer and more costly manufacturing process was without doubt better adapted to the equipment and machinery available at the G&R de Limoges factory and also to the quantities of steel available at that time.

If today it is not known who proposed these modifications, it seems evident that they came from a resistance fighter who had used the Sten and had been able to determine its weak points: a movable part allowing the bolt to be immobilized and thus avoiding gunfire if the weapon is accidentally dropped, the wooden butt made the shouldering of the weapon more comfortable , the forward grip gave the secondary hand a natural hold avoiding the temptation of holding the weapon by its magazine, and lastly, the longer barrel than on that of the original weapon contributed to its improved accuracy.

The manufacture of magazines was subcontracted to a factory in Brives, specializing in the bending and cutting of sheet metal, which made magazines of excellent quality. French-made magazines were distinct from British-made by the fact that the four magazine viewing holes were not drilled on the rear side of the magazine as on the Sten, but on the left side. These magazines, including the bottom plate, bear no markings and are phosphate coated and painted.

Rear view of the Gnome & Rhône R5.

Above, a Gnome & Rhône R5; below, a Sten Mk.II. In copying the Sten Mk.II, the workers at the Gnome & Rhône factory in Limoges were forced to remove certain faults of the British model by: improving the grip in the hand by the addition of a forward pistol grip, making the shouldering more comfortable with a wooden butt, and adding a part immobilizing the cocking handle forward so as to avoid accidental firing incidents. This example of the R5 is equipped with a Sten barrel. The original barrel was slightly longer.

The weapon itself presents a rough finish and is protected by parkerising in grey-green, not dissimilar to that found on some late-war German weapons. Perhaps the Limoges factory, forced to work for the occupier, had to carry out the surface treatments in accordance with German procedure?

The markings affixed on the top of the magazine housing are reduced to the minimum:

- The R5 marking of the fifth military region, which was later retained to designate the weapon in French military documents under the name "pistolet-mitrailleur Sten R5."
- A serial number, followed by a two-figure number, very probably indicating the month of manufacture.

The R5 submachine guns were first and foremost delivered to units encircling German pockets of resistance of the Atlantic wall in the southwest.

After the end of hostilities in Europe, the weapons of resistance were collected by the ordnance units of the French army in order to be reassigned to French forces undergoing reconstruction and, in particular, to units of the French expeditionary forces in the Far East and Indochina.

A chart pamphlet of collective units dated 1952, was still dedicated to the "*pistolet mitrailleur Sten R5 Gnome et Rhône de 9 mm.*" This period, near the end of the Indochina war, is when the French army had gradually begun to replace the heterogeneous equipment inherited from the Second World War with modern weapons from state-run factories, in order to rationalize both troop instruction and the supplies of ammunition and spare parts.

The British or French Stens, progressively replaced in the French units by MAT 49 submachine guns, were assigned to partisan units fighting against the Viet Minh alongside French troops.

A few Sten R5, which came back from Indochina or were kept in mainland units, were destroyed with other downgraded equipment at the end of the 1950s. The rarity of these weapons in both national and international collections is proof of their low survival rate during operations.

Butt of a Gnome & Rhône submachine gun. The principle of fixation to the receiver remains the same as on the Sten, but the butt is made up of a plate similar to those mounted on some German late-war weapons.

Marking on a magazine housing of a Gnome & Rhône submachine gun. An R5 marking can be seen under which is the number probably referring to the month of manufacture ("02" for February).

A Polish Version of the Sten: The *Blyskawika*

Unlike resistance movements of Western Europe and the Balkans, which benefitted from generous paradrops of weapons from the British, the Polish resistance, outside the range of SOE planes was for a long while meagerly armed. It was not until the end of 1943, when the Allies were able to take off from newly captured Italian airdromes, that they managed to carry out paradrops in Poland.

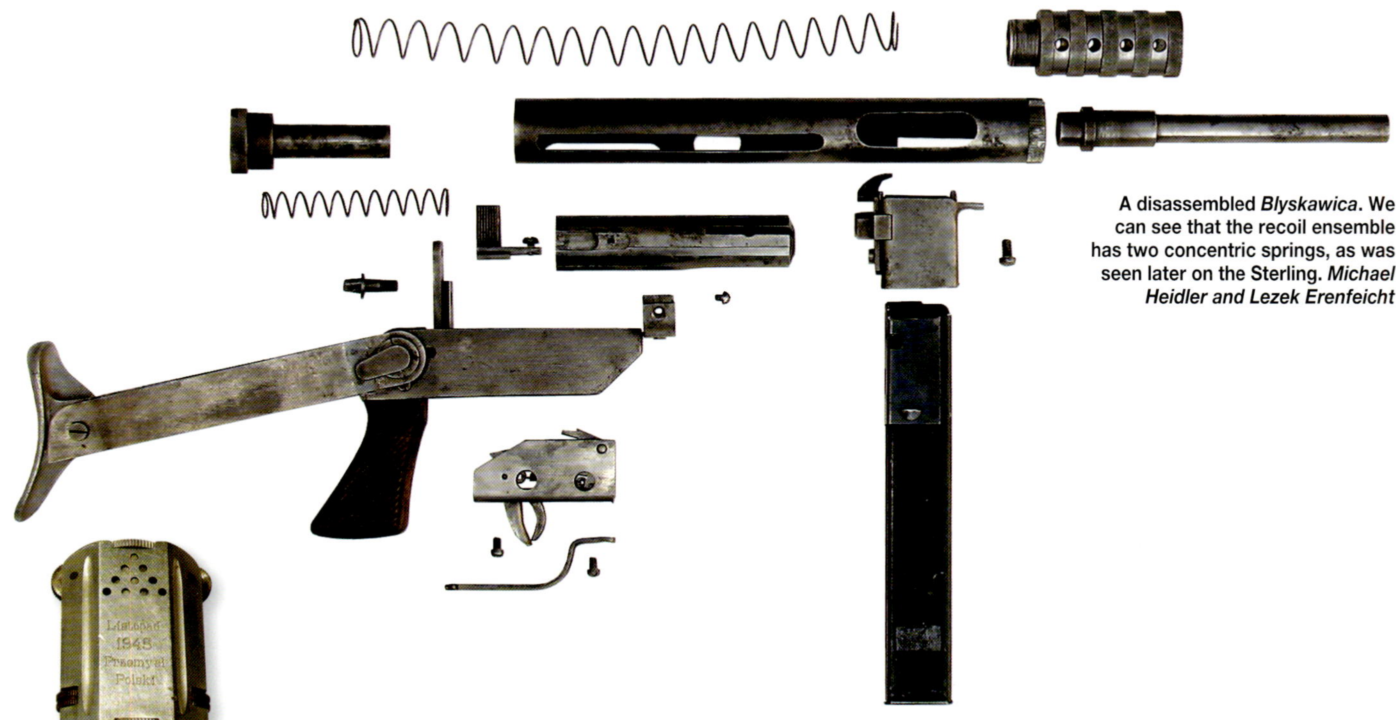

A disassembled *Blyskawica*. We can see that the recoil ensemble has two concentric springs, as was seen later on the Sterling. *Michael Heidler and Lezek Erenfeicht*

A commemorative lighter given to every participant in the manufacture of the *Blyskawica* on the occasion of the first delivery of these submachine guns to the secret army. Seweryn Wielanier, one of the creators of the weapon, was officially a manufacturer of petrol lighters. Each commemorative lighter is engraved with two expressions, which are only comprehensible for the initiated: "Polish Industry November 1943" on one side, and "lightning baptism" on the other. *Michael Heidler and Lezek Erenfeicht*

The USSR, which could have resupplied the Polish resistance or granted allied aircraft the authorization to stopover on its bases to refuel before returning to Great Britain, stubbornly refused any support to this non-communist resistance movement obedient to the Polish government in exile in London.

The Polish secret army (AK) eventually decided to manufacture covertly some submachine guns inspired by some MP40 removed from the *Wehrmacht*, a small number of parachuted Sten came to be added to that number.

Some small covert Polish workshops were already managing to make copies of the Sten. But the design of the weapon did not satisfy the Polish, as with its fixed butt and lateral magazine the weapon was difficult to conceal under clothing at the same time as keeping it ready to fire. In that respect it was better suited for combat in rural areas rather than for urban warfare.

In September 1942, the general staff of the AK who were preparing the Warsaw uprising made two mechanical engineers, Waclaw Zawrotny and Seweryn Wielanier, responsible for setting up a local and covert manufacture of a 9 mm caliber submachine gun. These engineers had no previous experience in weapons. After studying a Sten and an MP40 put at their disposal, the men came to the conclusion that the best solution would be to manufacture a weapon inspired by the Sten, for its simplicity of manufacture, but with a vertical magazine and a folding butt.

Considering the equipment and tools they had at their disposal they nonetheless chose to replace, by a simple screw arrangement, all bayonet mountings by a simple screw assembly, or by spring catches used on the Sten and MP40.

The first manufacturing plans were finished in April 1943. The setting up of production presented a real challenge as, at that time, the mechanical workshops were subject to strict checks by the occupying forces.

Moreover, the cutting tools, along with raw materials, were severely restricted and could only be bought by craftsmen benefitting from a special authorization from the German administration.

The clandestine manufacture of the *Blyskawica* was a real exploit due to the scarcity of raw materials and machine tools coupled with the close surveillance carried out in Warsaw by the German authorities. *Michael Heidler and Lezek Erenfeicht*

Despite these difficulties the two inventors, using stolen or embezzled materials or tools, managed to finish their first submachine gun prototype at the beginning of September 1943.

The board in charge of the equipment at the Polish underground army gave their approval to its adoption after test-firing carried out in the Zielonka woods in the suburbs of Warsaw.

The new weapon was christened "*Blyskawica*": meaning "lightning" in Polish and pronounced "*bouiskavitsa*." This name finds its origins in the three lightning bolts engraved on the weapon's aluminum butt plate. This relief of this engraving served to improve the grip and also to conceal the real use of this object officially identified as an "electric oven handle." The three lightning bolts were in fact the symbol of a brand of electrical equipment reputed in Poland at that time.

To commemorate the delivery of the first pre-production of five submachine guns** to the AK, all the main players that took part in the development of the weapon were given petrol lighters. These lighters were what Seweryn Wielanier officially made before dedicating himself to the covert manufacture of his submachine gun.

The Polish underground army ordered the assembly of 1,000 *Blyskawica* submachine guns, then placed a new order of 300 in July 1944. It seemed that in reality, only 600 weapons from the first order of 1,000 were in fact made, and that a hundred others were assembled afterwards during the preparation of the Warsaw uprising.

*** These five first weapons were destined to test the operation of manufacture networks and to be presented to resistance groups.*

The day after the surrender of Warsaw, this group of young combatants of the secret army pose for a souvenir photo before handing over the weapons to the enemy. On the *Blyskawica* seen here, the shortage of aluminum at the end of the siege meant the barrel machined in this metal had to be replaced by a simple steel ring. *Michael Heidler and Lezek Erenfeicht*

The bolt is a heavy breech block weighing 720 grams. Just like the bolt on the Sten, this part bears the grooves required for the movement of the ejector and the hooking of the trigger, as well as the introduction of the cocking handle. On the front, it has a fixed firing pin. Machined from a solid bar of steel and grooved lengthwise to reduce surface friction against the inside of the receiver. This arrangement is similar to that seen later on the bolts of some Sterling submachine guns. *Michael Heidler and Lezek Erenfeicht*

Blyskawica with a folded butt.
Michael Heidler and Lezek Erenfeicht

The three lightning bolts on the aluminum butt plate gave rise to its nickname.
Michael Heidler and Lezek Erenfeicht

Opposite page: Two 3008 submachine guns with *Volksturm* armbands, evoking the last movements of the war machine of the Third Reich. *Collection of the Royal Army Museum of Brussels and Le Poilu of Paris, Photo by Marc de Fromont*

The total number of submachine guns manufactured remains today the subject of passionate debate amongst amateur historians of Polish military history. The figure of 755 weapons is founded on the Polish underground army equipment inventory, some of which can be incomplete. The preservation of secrecy meant that accounting and bookkeeping were neglected in favor of total discretion.

Another estimation puts the total of only 555 *Blyskawicas* delivered to the Army. Whatever the real figure, and even taking the figure of 555, the manufacture of this quantity of *Blyskawica* submachine guns in the context mentioned above is a remarkable achievement!

Some *Blyskawicas* were concealed in rolls of wire fences and transferred to groups of resistance fighters set up in the east of Poland preparing for Operation Tempest, which was organizing a general uprising in the eastern provinces, with the intention of disrupting German transport and to facilitate the advance of the Red Army in Poland.

Unfortunately, Stalin, not wanting the slightest collaboration with the AK, decided to do things differently by creating the Polish government of Lublin on July 22, 1944, entirely devoted to the communists, and only recognized by the USSR. When the Warsaw uprising broke out on August 1, 1944, Stalin ordered the Red Army to stop its advance on the Vistula and to wait, arms at the ready, for the Germans to finish crushing the uprising organized by the Polish underground army. It was only once the non-communist resistance was crushed that the Soviet army started its advance towards the west again. The *Blyskawicas* not retrieved by the Germans when they attacked the maquis of the eastern regions were confiscated and destroyed after the war.

The manufacture of the *Blyskawica* ended on August 20, 1944, when the assembly workshop was destroyed by bombing. The last ones made bear witness to the scarcity of raw materials in the surrounded city; in addition they are generally stripped of their aluminum case, such a distinctive feature of this weapon.

In the context of dusty, urban guerilla warfare conducted during the Warsaw uprising, the weapons had to be cleaned very frequently. The use of small screws in the *Blyskawica* meant there was a risk of losing them during disassembly, whereas the fine threads serving to assemble the breech cover had to be kept scrupulously clean. Another flaw in the weapon lay in the aluminum barrel case which shone in the sun and often therefore made the users of the *Blyskawica* visible. The metal had been chosen because of its good heat conductivity supposed to facilitate cooling, but considering the lack of ammunition that the insurgents were subject to, the barrel overheating was extremely unlikely to happen. It is often the glare of the barrel case which identifies the existence of a *Blyskawica* when photos of the period are studied still today.

A single coat of matt paint could have made the barrel casing more discreet but it presented a second flaw resulting from its assembly of the receiver with find thread screws; the threads machined in the soft metal of aluminum deteriorated on contact with the steel of the receiver and meant it was difficult to hold the barrel correctly.

Certain photos dating from September or October 1944, show some *Blyskawica* where the barrel appears very bare as the case was replaced by a simple threaded washer probably in steel.

It is worth pointing out nonetheless that this weapon conceived by two men with no previous experience in armaments was a remarkable success, as much for its originality as for the marvel of organization required for its covert manufacture. Despite the difficult conditions of its production, its finish and assembly of parts are of the highest level. In a way, the *Blyskawica* well symbolizes the dominant characteristics of our Polish friends: patriotism, tenacity, courage, and ingenuity.

Group of insurgents in ambush in the ruins of Warsaw. One of them holds a Polish VIS 35 pistol, the other shoulders a *Blyskawica*. The aluminum cooling jacket around the barrel tended to lose its cover of black paint. The bright aspect of the aluminum rendered this weapon particularly visible! *Michael Heidler and Lezek Erenfeicht*

Trigger and safety pin. Unlike the Sten, the *Blyskawica* had no fire mode selector as the weight of the bolt imposed a slow firing speed, which easily permitted single shot firing if required by releasing the trigger between each shot. *Michael Heidler and Lezek Erenfeicht*

Im Dienst
der
Deutschen Wehrmacht
DEUTSCHER VOLKSSTURM
WEHRMACHT
Wehrpaß
Führerausweis
der
Hitler-Jugend

Certified copy of a Sten Mk.II, produced in the Mauser establishment under the name *"Gerät Potsdam,"* to equip future pro Nazi maquis in newly liberated regions. *Michael Heidler*

Detail of the magazine housing roughly welded on the receiver of a *"Gerät Potsdam." Michael Heidler*

SS-Gruppenführer Arthur Phleps, commander of the *"Prinz Eugen"* SS Division, examines a Sten Mk.II seized from the partisans. *DR*

German Copies of the Sten

At the end of the Second World War the German army was confronted with a serious shortage of submachine guns, attributable to several factors:

- following on from the change in situation concerning weapons on the eastern front, the seizure of, up until that point, abundant supplies of Soviet submachine guns diminished considerably, whereas the loss of weapons rose steeply.
- the production of MP40 was stopped in 1944, with a view to a general replacement of submachine guns in service by the MP43 assault rifle. Even though the German factories had delivered the *"Sturmgewehr"* within the time planned, the ammunition corresponding to the MP43 was not available in sufficient quantity to allow the distribution of assault rifles to all combatants.
- the advance of allied forces in north Italy interrupted the delivery of Beretta submachine guns, of which the *Wehrmacht* had captured great quantities.

In order to compensate for the lack of submachine guns, the *Wehrmacht* put Stens into service in its units, which had been captured from the maquis or from when the police of the *Reichssicherheitshauptamt* (RSHA: Reich Main Security Office) "placed an order" in Great Britain*** by the intermediary of captured resistance radio operators broadcasting under coercion.

The parachuted equipment seized served, first and foremost, to arm the auxiliary forces like the French militia. When the shortage of submachine guns occurred in 1944, as mentioned previously, the Stens were distributed to combat units of the *Wehrmacht.* However, this source of supply was not sustainable as the success of the allied landings in 1944, came with a reduction in the number of parachute drops and yet more seizures.

*** *The British were not totally deceived by these requests, but as they wanted to make the Germans believe that the landings would take place in the area of Boulogne sur Mer, they heavily supplied the networks in the north of France, even while knowing that the majority of their members had been captured by the enemy.*

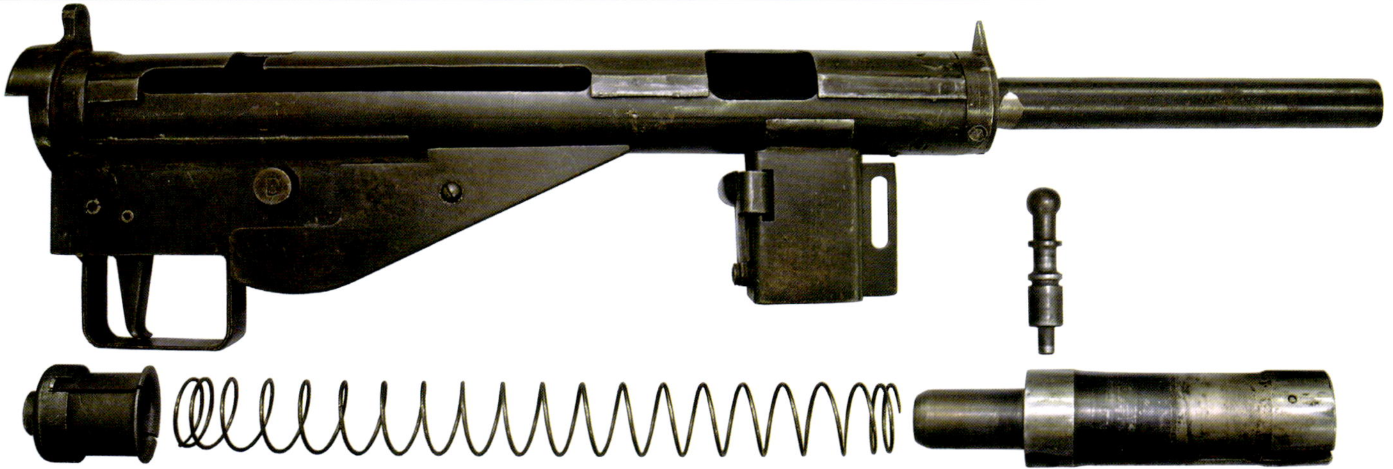

The mechanism of the MP3008 is faithfully copied from that of the Sten, but the barrel, mounted on the receiver, is not removable. *Prague Army Museum, photo by Michael Heidler*

Several perspicacious people in charge at the weapons ministry had understood that the prospect of the "final victory" was becoming more and more unlikely and that the increase of allied strategic bombing on Germany was going to inflict ever more ravages on industrial production. Thus, they were to develop secretly (to avoid the accusation of defeatism), a program of manufacturing simplified weapons (*primitivwaffen*), capable of being produced without sophisticated equipment and with the minimal use of raw materials, in small, scattered and not easily visible factories.

Concerning submachine guns, the British Sten appeared evidently to be the model to copy by the German industry committed to this new program. Two types of Sten copies were made:

1. Exact copies of the British Sten Mk.II, made in the Mauser establishment under the code name "*Gerät Potsdam*."

2. Extremely simplified copies of the Sten, which were christened MP3008, under the project code named "*Gerät Neumünster*."

The "*Gerät Potsdam*"

The care brought to the reproduction of the British weapon is explained by the fact that these weapons were destined to equip agents originally from the old occupied countries, who were, at the end of the war, following broadcasting and sabotage courses in German spy schools with the idea of being parachuted into liberated areas to create pro-Nazi maquis; It was in this context that the RSHA placed an order for 25,000 "*Gerät Potsdam*" submachine guns from the Mauser establishment. Before July 1944, the RSHA organized around 800 secret caches of weapons and equipment in occupied countries, from which parachuted agents could restock.

However, only several months from the fall of the III Reich, this plan of pro-German maquis met with very little support in liberated territory.****

Thomas B. Nelson points out in his work, *The World's Submachine Guns and Machine Pistols*, that the operation proved to be extremely costly as a credit of 1,800 *Reichsmarks* was given to Mauser by the RSHA for each copy made by the Mauser company. This sum represented approximately ninety times the price of an authentic British Sten!

**** *The agents parachuted were in general very young, having compromised themselves with the occupier and having followed the retreat of the Wehrmacht, once arrived in Germany had hardly any choice but to accept this type of mission. On their arrival in France, those who were not arrested by French counter-espionage had the good sense to disappear or emigrate.*

MP3008 submachine gun, also called the "*Gerät Neumünster*," an extremely simplified weapon against which a Sten Mk.II appears almost luxurious! *Prague Army Museum, photo by Michael Heidler*

Example of an MP3008 unusually fitted with a wooden butt. ***Michael Heidler***

Code "rde" roughly stamped on the receiver of an MP3008 made by the famous cutlery manufacturer Carl Eickhorn of Solingen. ***Michael Heidler***

For the sake of comparison, it should be noted that at the same time a K.98K rifle was invoiced at 28 *Reichsmarks*, and an MP43 at 80 *Reichsmarks*.

The manufacture of the "*Gerät Potsdam*" took place at the Mauser site in November and December 1944. The production was slightly less than 10,000 (9,972 to be precise). The majority of these weapons were concealed in hiding places organized by the secret services of the Reich in Germany and territories formerly occupied by the RSHA. Few of these hiding places have been located, therefore making the "*Gerät Potsdam*" very rare today.

The museum at Obendorf still conserves today an example of one of these "*Gerät Potsdam*" which is almost identical to a British Sten Mk.II. Only the method of making the magazine housing from a rough folded and welded on the underside differentiate a "*Gerät Potsdam*" from a British origin Sten.

A silencer, resembling a large tin box and fitted on the barrel was also made for these weapons.

During the course of an in-depth study on the subject of Sten submachine guns, Michel Moreau discovered an unusual example of "*Gerät Potsdam*." This weapon, on the surface identical to a Sten Mk.II, was made using traditional machining methods making it slightly heavier than "real" Stens. Moreover, on this example, the fire mode selector lever has the initials "D" and "E," indicating the functions of rapid fire and single shot fire ("*Dauerfeuer*" and "*Einzelfeuer*") in German instead of the letter "A" and "S" ("auto'" and "single") featuring on the selector lever of weapons of British manufacture, and the magazine housing is immobilized by a welded joint, and it accepts MP28 and not Sten magazines.

This second version of the "*Gerät Potsdam*" bears as its only marking a serial number: "50" and a small naval anchor struck on the stem of the "skeleton" butt. Mauser only made a part of the order so it is therefore possible to wonder if the remainder was entrusted to another manufacturer or if the weapon was due to be supplied to the *Wehrmacht*.

The "*Gerät Neumünster*" or MP3008

The *Wehrmacht*, informed of the existence of the "*Gerät Potsdam*" project developed for the RSHA, asked Mauser to conceive a simplified version of the "*Gerät Potsdam*" whose manufacture could potentially divided out between small companies so as to better escape allied aerial bombings.

To answer this request, one of the most talented inventors of the Mauser Company, Ludwig Vorgrimler, conceived a weapon inspired by the Sten, but lacking a pierced barrel nut. On this weapon the barrel was immobilized, during pressing, in the receiver before being permanently welded.

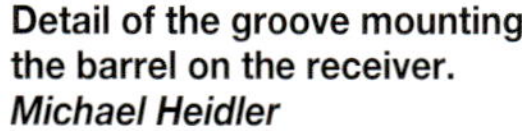

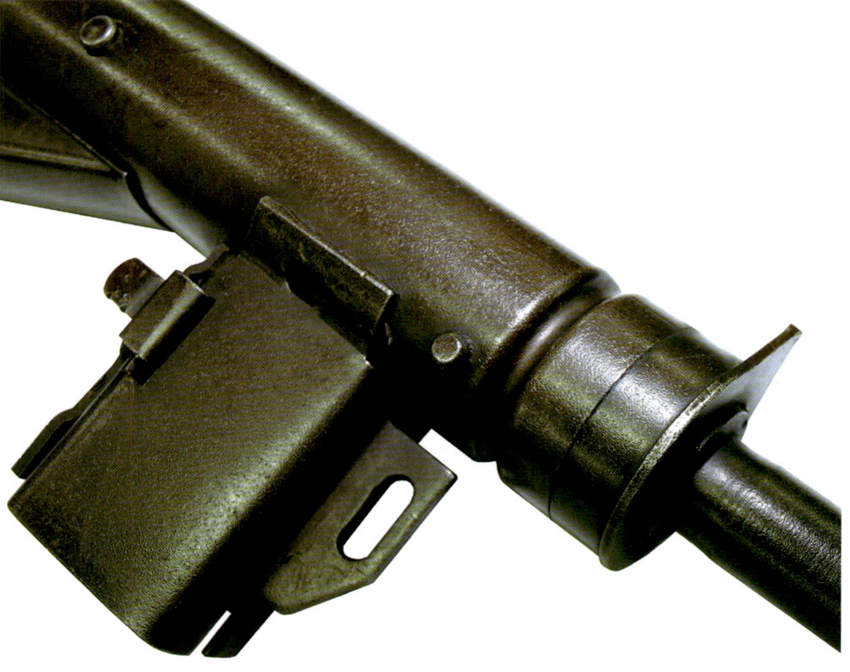

Detail of the groove mounting the barrel on the receiver. ***Michael Heidler***

The receiver itself was formed from a rolled sheet of metal, welded at the front and back. The bolt handle slid in the groove formed in the central, non-welded part.

The magazine housing was no longer horizontal and mobile as on the Sten, but vertical and welded.

The time required to make a "*Gerät Neumünster*" was estimated at one hour. The weapon was fed by an MP40 magazine. The first submachine guns of this type were equipped with a flat wooden butt, then a butt in "T," copied from the No.2 butt of the Sten but where the grip was without the circular cut that is seen on butts on English weapons.

Subsequently, these weapons were mounted with "skeleton" butts relatively similar to the No.3 butt mounted on some British Stens.

This second project, aiming to develop a simplified version of the Sten, was called by the code name of "*Gerät Neumünster*."

In the classification of the *Waffenamt*, the weapon received the reference number (*Gerät Nummer*): "1-3-3008" which brought about the name "MP3008" after the war.

However, just as W. Darrin Weaver mentions in his book, *Desperate Measures*, dedicated to weapons of the *Volksturm*, this submachine gun was called simply "*Volksmachinenpistole*" by official nazi authorities and "*Sten Maschinenpistole*" by its users.

It seems that Mauser first of all made two examples of "*Gerät Neumünster*." They were presented to the German technical services that tested them and gave a favorable opinion to begin mass production after having several minor modifications carried out. Once the green light was given, it would seem Mauser had a small series of around 150 examples made, destined to be taken up as the model for the factories involved in the "*Volksmachinenpistole*" manufacturing program.

Weaver determined that there were fourteen assembly centers receiving components made by thirty or so factories working as sub-contractors.

This abundance of manufacturing points explains the slight differences in detail that can be seen today between the various MP3008s.

The MP3008 results initially from an order from the German army (*Heer*), destined to arm regular troops and not, contrary to what a lot of authors thought prior to the publication of Weaver's book, from an order from the Nationalist Socialist party to arm the *Volksturm*.

Once the production destined for the army was started, another production of these submachine guns was also ordered by the Nazi government for the *Volksturm*.

Among the weapons coming out of the same factory at the same time, there were those that were stamped with a manufacturer's code, the initial "H" of the army that bore the inspection stamp of the *Waffenamt*, whereas others bore no markings other than the number. The current theory is that the first were destined for regular troops of the *Wehrmacht* and the second for the *Volksturm*.

Various other companies took part in the manufacture of the MP3008 or some of its elements but the list of these companies remains today very difficult to establish with certainty as much archive material of this period has been destroyed or lost. The researchers who study this weapon are also hindered by the fact that certain codes on some weapons cannot be attributed.

The extremity of a cocking handle on most MP3008 have a spherical shape. *Michael Heidler*

The assemblers of the MP3008 identified today are as follows:

- C.G. Haenel Waffen-und Fahrradfabrik (code "fxo")
- ERMA produced, it seems, some MP3008 components but not complete weapons
- W.J. Hölzen (code not identified)
- Gottfried Linder A.G. (code "dxl")
- Gustav Appel: a company set up in Spandau, well known for its RG34 cleaning kits that it supplied in great quantity to the *Wehrmacht* throughout the entire war (code "cnx")
- Gerhard & Schubert, of Amberg (code "DCO")
- Gerhard Glos und Voll, of Würtzburg (code not identified)
- Walther Steiner of Stuhl (code "nea")
- Blohm & Voss: great naval shipyard in Hamburg, Blohm & Voss had to manufacture submachine guns after allied bombs completely destroyed its heavy installations. The Blohm & Voss submachine guns have a different appearance to other 3008 submachine guns: the rear of the barrel is surrounded by a perforated cooling case. They are in addition equipped with either a flat wooden butt or a "T" butt with a pistol grip. These weapons are marked with the initials of the firm; "B&V" inside two circles.
- Karl Eickhorn. This Solingen cutlery firm, with strong links to the Nazi party, seems to have produced only twenty-six MP3008s (code "RDF") before the arrival of the Allies (code "cof" and possibly "RDE" at the end of the war).

Unidentified "tjg" code of a manufacturer in the Hamburg region, which took part in the production of MP3008. The marking "45" can also be seen indicating the year of manufacture. *Michael Heidler*

Belgian soldiers armed with Sten submachine guns photographed in the immediate aftermath of the war. *Patrick Denamur*

Moreover non-identified codes such as "tjg," "tvw," or "TJK" have been noted on some MP3008, without their manufacturer being identified.

There are some slight differences between the MP3008 depending on their manufacturer. The finish of these weapons goes from the purely functional to the frankly execrable. The weapon gives off a certain fragility accentuated yet more on certain makes by a rattling of the magazine in its housing which, by contrast, gives the Sten the appearance of a luxury submachine gun.

Between November 1944, and April 1945, it is estimated that 3,000 to 5,000 MP3008 submachine guns were made in the territory of the Reich.

Taking in to account the circumstances and the diversity of manufacturers, there are some slight differences.

Just like the "*Gerät Potsdam*," the MP3008 seem to have mysteriously disappeared. Few weapons of this type have been found, the others having been either buried in hiding places organized for the resistance movements (*Wehrwolf*) that the Nazi party hoped to see develop in Allied-conquered zones, or destroyed by the bombing, or possibly also destroyed by their manufacturers before the arrival of the Allies.

Belgian Stens*

The Sten submachine gun made its appearance in the Belgian military arsenal after the war. The Belgian army of this period was equipped with a great number of British-origin weapons. Indeed, the Belgian government, evacuated to England, had mobilized Belgians residing abroad to carry on the fight against the German invader. All parts of the British armed forces, from the RAF to the Royal Navy, therefore, had Belgians in their ranks. The infantry had the possibility of expressing their talents in the commandos or the famous *Brigade Piron* (the name of its commanding officer).

* *Text: Patrick Denamur.*

Markings on a Belgian Sten:

- "AsArm" is the mark of the Rocourt weapons arsenal.
- "ABL" is a bilingual mark, meaning "armée belge/ Belgische Leger" which appears on the majority of regulation Belgian weapons.
- "51" is of course the date of manufacture. The diamond-shaped symbol is the logo of the Grimaud company of Liege.

Unlike British Stens, the weapon serial number is found on the main parts of the mechanism. *Patrick Denamur*

Two Sten Mk.II presenting the two types of regulation finishes for the Belgian army: one painted in black, the other in matt grey. The type of finish depends on the period of manufacture rather than being specific to a particular weapon. *Patrick Denamur*

Two Sten Mk.IIs of the Belgian army photographed with equipment of Belgian para-commandos, along with Belgian cartridge boxes, a cleaning kit, and a magazine pouch with eight compartments much used by airborne troops. *Collection of the Royal Army Museum of Brussels and Patrick Denamur, Photo by Marc de Fromont*

Belgian proof stamp on a mobile bolt. *Patrick Denamur*

Belgian soldiers equipped and armed with British Sten, Bren and Enfield, photographed during a water exercise. *Patrick Denamur*

Belgian Sten are equipped with an Mk.III butt in which a cleaning rod is fixed by clips. *Patrick Denamur*

"Bg" marking on a Sten magazine indicating Belgian manufacture from material of foreign origin. The "P" in a circle is the logo of the Assenmaker-Outil Press company. *Patrick Denamur*

All the Sten models were in use, more or less intensively, after the war. Even though the Mk.I model appears in manuals of the period, no iconography known shows it in service in the Belgian army. The Mk.V and the Mk.II S however were used by the Para-Commando regiments. Evidently, it is the Mk.II and Mk.III that are found most often in the weapons racks of the units.

At the beginning of the fifties, national weapon production was relaunched: Mauser model 24/30 rifle, AFN and SAFN, FM type D, and PM Vigneron. Curiously, the adoption of a new submachine gun did not cause the Sten to be consigned to oblivion in the mobilization stores. Quite the opposite, a production of new weapons was launched calling on private manufacturers. But, for all that, the old weapons from the Second World War stock were not abandoned; on the contrary they were thoroughly renovated by the arsenal at Rocourt.

To date, three Belgian manufacturers of this weapon have been identified:

- the Imperia company, which after building automobiles in the inter-war period, tried to diversify its production after a vain attempt to manufacture the Volkswagen "Beetle" in its Nesonvaux factories (near Liege). It is not known what brought this ambitious project to an end, but the financial reason is the most onerous!

  During the trials of a new submachine gun, this firm had proposed a hybrid weapon, one being a Beretta 38A wooden casing in conjunction with a Sten mechanism; a sort of luxury Sten. This daring project did not come to anything; the firm was eventually called upon to make Sten Mk.II submachine guns true copies of British models.

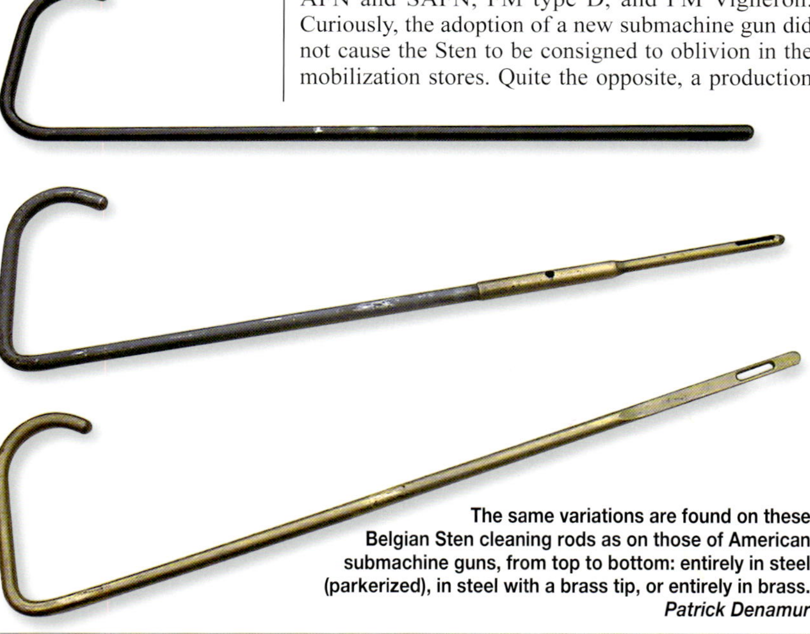

The same variations are found on these Belgian Sten cleaning rods as on those of American submachine guns, from top to bottom: entirely in steel (parkerized), in steel with a brass tip, or entirely in brass. *Patrick Denamur*

The "Austen" submachine gun, an Australian version of the Sten, equipped with a folding butt and a recoil spring telescopic casing, as on the German MP40. *Michael Heidler*

- the Grimaud establishment also manufactured Sten Mk.II submachine guns. This firm, created in 1908, still exists today although no longer makes weapons; it has now reoriented itself to the import of weapons and accessories. Aside from the manufacture of Sten, Grimaud also manufactured small spare parts for the upkeep and maintenance of the Bren light machine guns and Vickers machine guns, among others, in use in the Belgian army.

- the firm Outil-Press. This other supplier of the Belgian army was also a partner in the adventure of the Belgian Sten. The Sten Mk.II submachine gun spare parts made by Outil-Press were delivered to Imperia and Grimaud for final assembly. This company also delivered spare parts for numerous weapons and ammunition to the Belgian army, among them magazines for the Lee-Enfield No.4, SAFN bayonet covers, .30-06 caliber ammunition clips, small parts and magazines for the Vigneron submachine gun, two-inch mortar shell, small maintenance box kits, etc. In the mid-fifties the issue of Vigneron submachine guns came to an end and, for the most part, the Stens were allocated to reserve units. Nonetheless, the light Avi (Land Army helicopters) used this legendary weapon up to 1985. The Sten was then replaced in the services by FNC rifles.

Presentation of the Weapon

On first inspection the only thing which differentiates a Sten Mk.II ABL from its British counterpart is the presence of a cleaning rod fitted in the skeleton butt of the weapon. It is well known that the rigor of peacetime service necessitated a more thorough cleaning of the weapon. Another annoyance in peacetime was the numbering components; the barrel or its case, the butt, the bolt (stamped with a number and engraved with an electric engraving pen). As for the body, this bore the weapon number both on its magazine housing and on the trigger guard, even though these two parts cannot normally be separated by a user!

It is possible to come across weapons that bear a second, different number on the magazine housing, this indicates the weapon was allocated to the Ministry of Finance (Belgian customs motorcycle brigade), which numbered the equipment for its inventory.

Stens of the Pacific: Australia and New Zealand

As soon as the Sten Mk.II was in active use in Great Britain, specimens of the weapon, along with technical documentation were sent to the principal Dominions: Canada, Australia, and New Zealand in particular, so the local armies could become familiar with the weapon and to allow these countries to examine the setting up of local manufacturers.

For Australia and New Zealand, the Japanese threat did not really materialize until after December 7, 1941, the date of the attack on the American base at Pearl Harbor, which constituted the prelude to a widespread offensive by Japanese forces in Asia and the Pacific.

As far as Australia was concerned, the specimens of Sten sent from Great Britain in 1941, had been carefully studied, but as the country was not at war, the Australians had the bad idea of wanting to do better than the home country by developing an improved version of the Sten, one which conserved the key features, but was equipped with a folding butt and a recoil spring contained in telescopic tubes based on the design of the German MP38 submachine gun.

Marking on the magazine housing of an Austen. *MRA collection*

A Dutch–Moluccan detachment armed with Austens surrounding an Indonesian nationalist prisoner. *DR*

Australian parachutist equipped with an Austen. *DR*

These studies seriously delayed the manufacture of the Sten, so Australian soldiers confronted by the Japanese offensive on New Guinea did not have submachine guns at their disposal apart from a few Thompson brought from the USA. Faced with this urgent situation the Australian government placed an order with a private company in Port Kembla for an unusual submachine gun: the Owen.

The weapon had been developed manually by a very young man, Edwin Owen, who had made a prototype of a .22LR caliber submachine gun in his father's garage before 1939. It was presented to the technical services of the Australian army in Sydney in July 1939, but only received mild interest at the time. After this unfortunate experience, Owen went on to enlist as a soldier in the Australian army.

However, Vincent Wardell, an industrialist friend of his father who had examined Owen's prototype in 1939, used his influence to have Owen posted to a department dealing with the development of new weapons. From that moment on, Owen took over the development of his submachine gun, this time in an official capacity. He equipped his weapon with a magazine vertically positioned over the receiver. This arrangement, common on light machine guns but less so on submachine guns, was however, judicious, as a magazine of more than twenty rounds positioned under the weapon would inevitably be an obstruction for firing in a lying down position and would force the shooter to reveal his position.

Tool for loading magazines on an Austen, based on that of a Sten.

Disassembled Austen. An obvious resemblance between the bolt-recoil spring ensemble on the Austen and the MP40. *Michael Heidler*

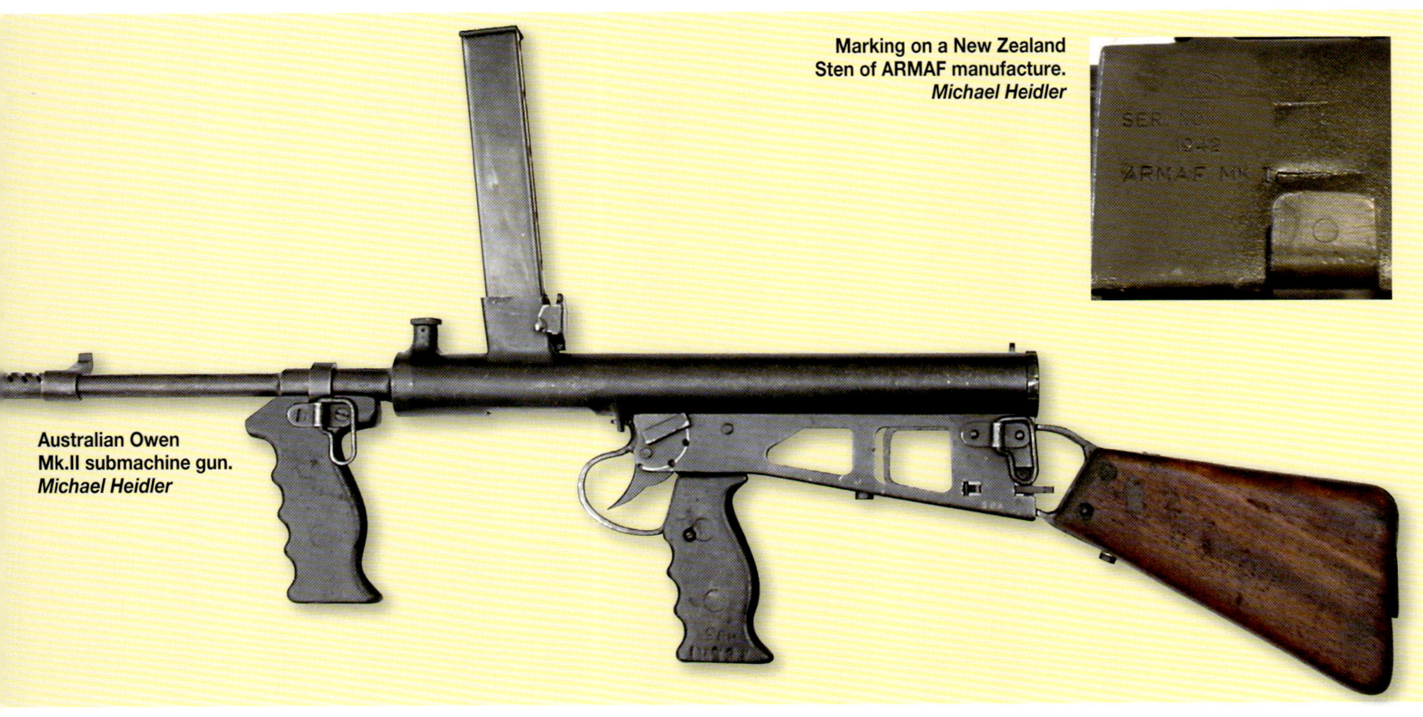

Marking on a New Zealand Sten of ARMAF manufacture. *Michael Heidler*

Australian Owen Mk.II submachine gun. *Michael Heidler*

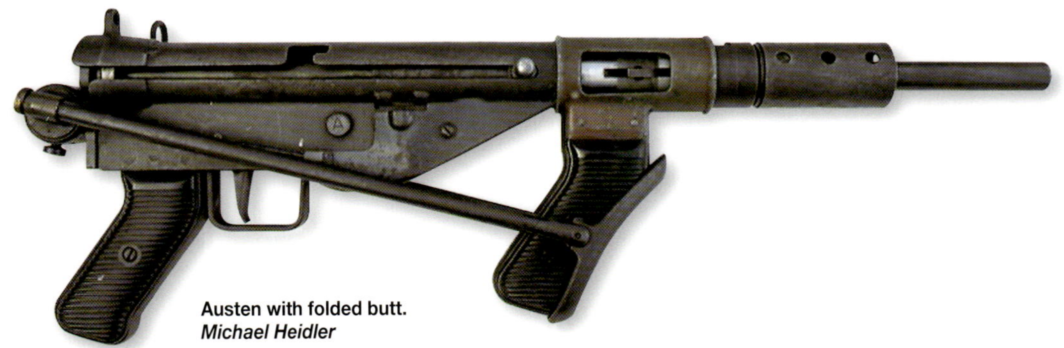

Austen with folded butt. *Michael Heidler*

Lateral magazines, like those found on the Sten, do not have this disadvantage but, being long, they can get caught up during advances in dense undergrowth, whereas a vertical magazine positioned on top of the weapon (as on some light-machine guns) is in line with the chest of the shooter and is not an obstruction. In addition, the magazine spring does not have to counter the weight of the column of cartridges but only to regulate and accelerate the descent by gravity, which facilitates the supply of cartridges to the weapon.

On the Owen submachine gun, the rear side of the magazine was cut out in such a way as to act as an ejector tab. Even though he was assigned to a military organization, Edwin Owen, still considering himself ethically and morally the owner of the weapon, filed a patent to protect the mechanism in July 1941. Owen signed an agreement, most likely through the intermediary of Vincent Wardell, with the aim of manufacturing it with the John Lysagh company of Port Kembla.

Owen's prototype, tested in the worst environmental conditions together with a Sten and a Thompson, proved to be the most resistant of the weapons when immersed in liquid mud. Australia, under threat of a Japanese invasion from 1942, started to reconsider its indifference to submachine guns and placed an order for a first batch of 200 Owen submachine guns with the John Lysagh company.

The design of the Owen made its manufacture very easy, but the conditions of production at Lysagh, a metal works at Port Kembla, did not make it possible to ensure the interchangeability of parts, which had to be adjusted in the event of replacement.

A defect in the first batches of 9 mm Parabellum made in Australia delayed the release for service of the Owen submachine gun. But once the problem of cartridges was resolved the weapon was used in combat in New Guinea against the Japanese, and it rapidly gained great popularity amongst Australian soldiers.

Edwin Owen with some of his submachine guns. ***DR***

Both the Australian and New Zealand armies placed new orders, which took the total number of Owens made between 1942 and September 1944, to approximately 45,000. Unlike the Sten, the Owen is made from a thick-lined metal tube, which made it heavy (4.2 kg empty and 4.8 kg loaded). Just like the Sten, however, the Owen had a non-fixed bolt operation. Both its 24.5 cm length barrel and the butt could be dismantled manually. The total length of the weapon was 81.5 cm. Two pistol grips made it easy to hold during firing.

The Owen had several versions:

- Mk.I equipped with a ribbed barrel
- Mk.II with a non-ribbed barrel but composed of two cylindrical portions of different diameters
- Mk.III identical to the Mk.III but with a section of longer and thicker barrel

These three variations went together with three variations of butt:

- Mk.I steel (entirely metal)
- Mk.I wood (butt in solid wood)
- Mk.I Wood Lightened. In solid wood with milled parts in its central section

After the war, the Australian army kept the Owen in service until the F1 submachine gun was taken up around 1960. The weapon was also used by the Australian contingents, engaged in Korea and Vietnam, alongside the Americans. During anti-guerilla operations in Malaysia, the British SAS also adopted the Owen as a replacement for the Sten Mk.V which functioned less reliably in the jungle. The Austen, eventually adopted in 1942, started its manufacture slowly, and only 19,914 were made by Diecasters Ltd. of Melbourne, and W.T. Carmichael Ltd., of Sydney.

Stens of New Zealand

Two New Zealand companies manufactured the Sten:

- Precision Engineering Co. Ltd. (marking ARMAF Mk.I)
- Radio Corporation of New Zealand (marking LP for Local Pattern)

The receiver on the New Zealand "LP" Sten is made from rolled sheet metal and welded in its upper section. The welded section forms a strip on the upper part of the tube, as what was seen later on the Mk.III model. The magazine housing is fixed, but the barrel can still be dismantled. Some elements, therefore, are found on this weapon that link it to the Mk.II and others to the Mk.III.

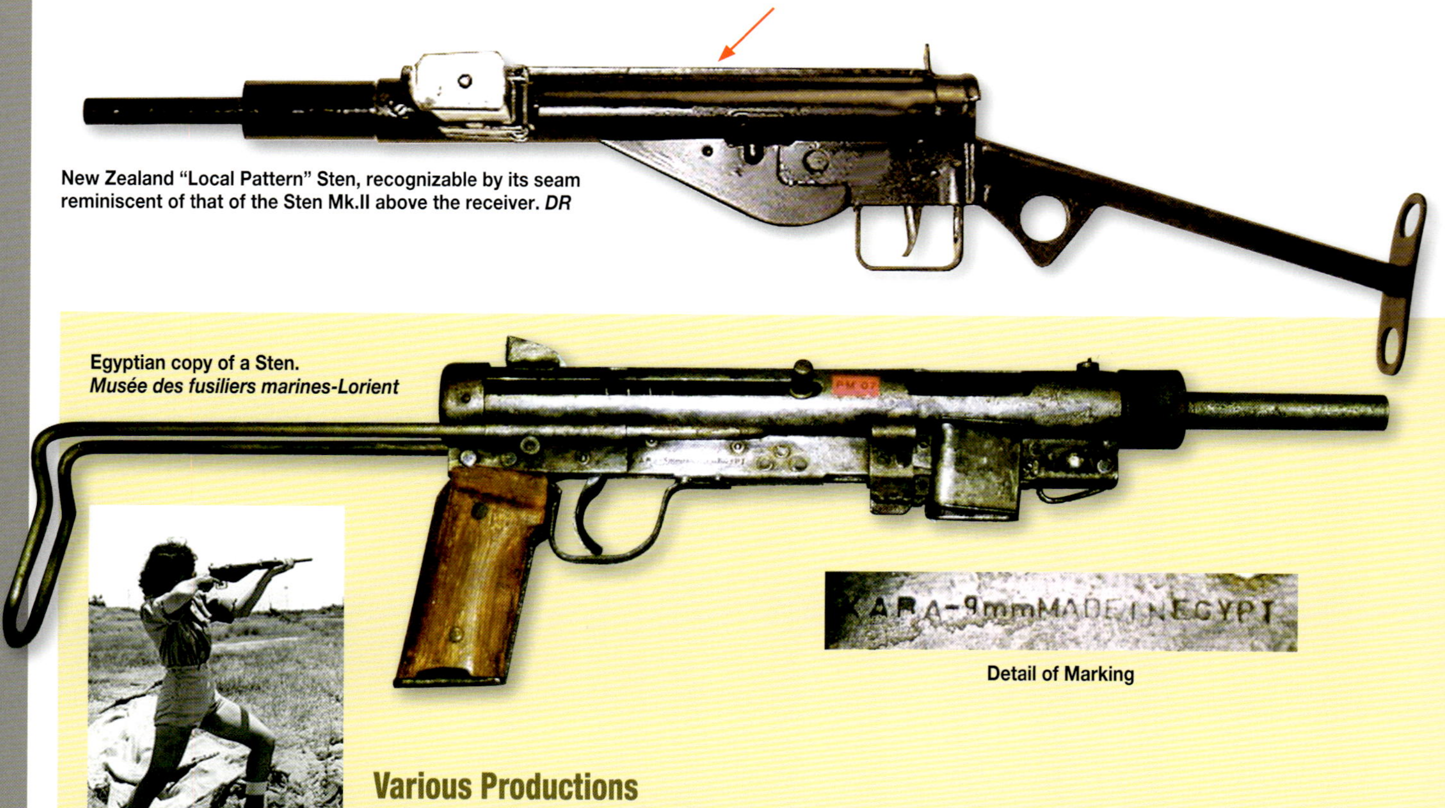

New Zealand "Local Pattern" Sten, recognizable by its seam reminiscent of that of the Sten Mk.II above the receiver. ***DR***

Egyptian copy of a Sten.
Musée des fusiliers marines-Lorient

Detail of Marking

Young Israeli combatant photographed with a Sten during the 1948 war of independence. ***DR***

Various Productions

Able to be produced in any mechanical workshop, the Sten submachine gun was a weapon of choice for all guerilla and resistance fighters. During the Second World War, Danish and Norwegian resistants were producing them under the nose of the occupier. After the Second World War, Zionist organizations made Stens in Palestine, and Viet Minh underground workshops made them in Indochina. In 1991, after the beginning of the war that was to lead to the dividing up of Yugoslavia, the Croat insurgents made, in a makeshift way initially and later with a more sophisticated approach, submachine guns whose mechanism was based on the Sten (the Pletter and Zagi). The principle of the Sten had a long career, and it is doubtless the progressive discontinuation of submachine guns in favor of assault rifles that brought it to an end.

CONCLUSION

Lt. Col. Gambiez, commando of the first French groupement de choc, photographed with a Sten during the winter of 1944, during fighting in Franch-Comte. This photograph is posed; even though he appears to be pressing the trigger, the cocking handle is at safety. *ECPAD*

The Sten today remains tarnished with an ambivalent reputation, very certainly influenced by the memories of certain members of the resistance who were allocated one. The negative comments are of several types:

- **Physical aspect**. Opening the first parachuted containers, many resistance fighters were very disappointed with the basic appearance of the Sten delivered to them. For those men who had known pre-war weapons, carefully finished and man-machined, the Sten could indeed appear disconcerting. The appearance of the Thompson, MP40 of "Moscheto Automatico" Beretta was much more flattering! However, although the Beretta was the best of the bunch, the combatant kitted out with a Sten with good magazines and cartridges was not really at a disadvantage when faced with a bearer of a Thompson or an MP40.

- **Safety aspect**. Principally linked to the operation of the inertia breech block and the absence of a really reliable security system. A strong impact, such as being dropped on the butt, could be enough to make the bolt move back, remove a cartridge in the magazine, and strike it after being pushed towards the front by the recoil spring. It seems that this defect was the cause of numerous accidents. To avoid this type of problem, it was advised to carry the weapon with the bolt at the rear, the bolt handle attached to the safety catch. This security was sometimes uncertain, however, so the adoption of the Mk.5 safety lever at the end of 1944, which simply needed to be pushed to immobilize the magazine firmly, represented real progress. Unfortunately, the majority of Sten parachuted to the French maquis were not yet provided with this system, which became widespread on Stens kept in service after the war.

Another type of accident occurred when the user used weakly loaded cartridges:* the bolt did not go back sufficiently to attach to the trigger, but far enough to take off a new cartridge in the magazine after the shot was fired and ignite. All rounds contained in the charger could thus be fired inadvertently. If the user was not very experienced (common among young resistance fighters), he ran the risk of panicking and spraying shots all around him instead of keeping his weapon in a line until the magazine was empty. This type of incident was also related by credible witnesses concerning Italian partisans who had the recklessness to fill a Sten magazine with 9 mm Glisenti cartridges which did not have a strong enough charge to ensure a sufficient recoil to connect the bolt and the trigger.

A highly symbolic weapon, the Sten appears in many monuments commemorating the resistance: here a monument to the partisans of Parma. *DR*

Aperitif for the maquis: an eternal image of France! In the middle of the group, two Sten Mk.IIs are placed on the table. The cocking handle of the gun on the left is hooked to the safety catch, conforming to regulation use of the weapon. *DR*

Full page opposite: Equipment and uniform of a Polish lieutenant parachutist in Holland (September 1944), with his Sten Mk.II with skeleton butt. *Photo by Marc de Fromont*

- **Frequent jamming incidents.** Although no more frequent than on other submachine guns fed by Schmeisser type magazines. On this type of magazine, the cartridges, initially arranged in two interlocking columns, become progressively one as they get nearer to the lips of the magazine. It resulted in friction that disrupted the correct advancement of the cartridges. If the distance between the lips had not been adjusted correctly or had been damaged slightly the cartridge could become blocked in the magazine and jam the weapon. This type of incident is also fostered by the filling of the magazines at the theoretical capacity of thirty-two cartridges: in this case, the pressure of the column of cartridges on the magazine lips is too great and hinders the bolt taking up the cartridge. That is why it was recommended not to fill the magazines with more than twenty-eight rounds. A common mistake of badly trained shooters was to hold the weapon by the magazine that also led to "feeding" incidents.

- **Lack of accuracy.** This is a false accusation: the weapon is very accurate in single shot and continuous burst fire, provided that, for the Sten Mk.II, the barrel chisel mark is in the correct position. Moderate firing speed rendered the weapon particularly easy to control, and the eyesight, even though it was basic, offered a much better aim than the open notch sight on the German MP40.

The majority of failings attributed to the Sten, it can be concluded, could therefore be corrected by proper training of the user: a condition often difficult to fulfil for a weapon destined to be parachute dropped to guerrilla units!

On the other hand the weapon was light, easy to disassemble and maintain, and could be disassembled in several parts, the longest of which measured no more than 33 cm (for the Mk.II model, which was the most common for the maquis), this facilitated its concealment and transport in enemy occupied territory. In particular, the weapon, produced in abundance and at low cost, could be parachuted without economy in mind and therefore the necessity of following closely the movements of resistance fighters.

In the end, the legendary German MP40, which so often was set against the Sten, was hardly superior to it. Its only objective advantage resided in the existence of a folding butt. It seems important to set the record straight about a weapon, often unfairly denigrated and which, it must be remembered, gave a great service to France and today is seen as a symbol of the resistance.

German Submachine Guns, 1918–1945
Bergmann MP18/I • MP34/38/40/41 • MKb42/43/1
MP43/1 • MP44 • StG44 • Accessories
978-0-7643-5486-1

American Submachine Guns, 1919–1950
Thompson SMG • M3 "Grease Gun"
Reising • UD M42 • Accessories
978-0-7643-5484-7

CLASSIC GUNS OF THE WORLD SERIES